WORKING FERRETS

Selection, Training and Sport

Jackie Drakeford

SWAN·HILL
PRESS

Copyright Text © 1996 Jackie Drakeford
Copyright Photographs © 1996 Phillip Blackman and Jackie Drakeford

First published in the UK in 1996
by Swan Hill Press, an imprint of Airlife Publishing Ltd.

British Library Cataloguing in Publication Data
   A catalogue record for this book
   is available from the British Library

ISBN 1 85310 804 9

Typeset by Phoenix Typesetting, Ilkley, West Yorkshire
Printed in England by Livesey Ltd, Shrewsbury

Swan Hill Press
an imprint of Airlife Publishing Ltd
101 Longden Road, Shrewsbury SY3 9EB, England

To all the gamekeepers, farmers, landowners and agents by whose grace I hunt.

Acknowledgements

Special thanks are due to Derek Homden for making time in a busy schedule to provide the ferret drawings; to Phillip Blackman for his unflagging encouragement and help; to Sarah Smith, Dave Smithers, Angie Dear and John Dear for their assistance with the photographs; to Jo Lundgren and Dave Lovatt for allowing me unlimited ferreting; to Jack Russell for practical advice, and to the GEM Ferret Care Group for all that they do for ferrets and ferreters.

CONTENTS

Chapter One

Introduction To Ferreting

What does ferreting involve? What is a bury, and what different sorts are there? What goes on above ground, what happens below, what do you need, what do you wear, *how do you do it?*

There is a lot of mystique to ferreting, but no mystery. Think like a ferret, think like a rabbit, and learn to read the land that you have walked over daily without a thought. There are excellent books that will tell you how ferrets came to these islands, and how to feed, house, breed and tend them – this book is not one of them. It covers working the ferret to rabbit, its primary quarry, in all the different ways that we can. Having read your care and maintenance books, you may be ready to acquire your first ferrets and your ferreter's starter kit. But before you do, enjoy a few days' ferreting through these pages.

1

Whatever methods you use to capture the rabbits once they leave the bury, the technique for getting them to do so is the same. Give your ferrets a light snack before you leave home – an egg, a small piece of meat each, a teaspoonful of dry food, for instance. If fully fed, a ferret will only want to sleep, and if hungry it will eat any rabbit it kills underground and then sleep off the meal, which is called a lie-up. No more rabbits will be bolted until you have dug down to the sleeping ferret, and when you do, you will find a mangled rabbit that is only fit for ferret food. There is quite enough digging in store for you without asking for more, so give your co-hunters breakfast before you start out. It helps to keep the carrying box clean if you give your ferrets enough time to attend to their ablutions after they have eaten, and I keep a spare hutch for this purpose, as they cannot resist 'marking' unfamiliar territory. The best way of training any animal is to go along with its natural instincts: ferrets are very clean, and they are happier and much pleasanter to handle if you help them to stay that way.

Now for your own preparation: think rabbit. They do not have big eyes, long ears and twitching noses for nothing. Their senses are far keener than ours, and rabbits are under threat from predators every hour of their lives. So, if they know that you are outside their bury, even if a ferret is inside their home with them, they will be very reluctant to bolt and face an unknown danger when they can stay on familiar ground and face a known one. To avoid alerting the rabbits to your presence, you need to be quiet in your movements, sober in your dress, and careful not to introduce alien scents into their perception. This means no smoking, no peppermints, and no perfume or aftershave. Clothes should enable you to move easily and quietly, and should match the greens and browns of the countryside. A rabbit may hop to the very entrance of a hole and sit still, testing for safety; should you be wearing your sparkling white T-shirt and bright red jeans, you will not fit into the rabbit's preferred scheme of scenery. Scientists at the beginning of this century insisted that animals could not see colour; this theory has since been roundly disproved, and if you are wearing bright colours, the rabbit will see you. If it sees you, it will not bolt, and you will end up digging again when it could have been avoided.

Rabbiting clothes will soon suffer from the corrosive effects of mud, blood and rabbit urine, so do not wear anything that you are fond of. You will get hooked up on barbed wire, surprised by electric fencing, spattered with cow dung, and possibly drenched in smelly water when you inadvertently step backwards into a brook, so wear tough clothes that can be washed without compromise. Turn out the pockets regularly to avoid unpleasant surprises, and be prepared to replace your ferreting clothes every year or so. Always wear a hat. It will keep your head warm, mask the shine of a bald head, protect you from scratches from brambles and holly – and it is something to wring nervously in your hands when you have not seen your ferret for an hour! Most of us favour a flat tweed cap, but try out a few different sorts and see which you like best.

When the ferret enters the first rabbit hole, look at your watch. Often nothing will happen for quite a while, and it is amazing how long twenty minutes can seem, so note the time before your start. It is also good for ferreters' tales down at the pub along the lines of 'We had twenty-one rabbits in half an hour.' Probably no one will believe you, and quite right too. Nevertheless, always note the time. Then keep still, out of direct line of sight from the rabbit holes. There is a lot more to being quiet than not talking; do not jingle change, rustle sweet papers, blow your nose, cough or sneeze. Do not shuffle your feet – the rabbits can feel the vibration of your movements through the earth. If you are ferreting with the aid of a dog, remember that the dog is following movement underground by listening, scenting, and feeling; anything that you add in the way of noise or movement is distracting and irritating to her, making her job much harder.

When the rabbits start to bolt, you will be working frantically. You will have to pick up the netted rabbit, put your foot in the rabbit hole to stop the next one bolting up your shirt, despatch the rabbit as quickly as possible – there are several good ways, and I will discuss all of them, so that you can decide which suits you best – set another net over the hole, and put the dead rabbit down well away from any rabbit holes. The sight and smell of recently killed rabbits will dissuade others from bolting, and your ferret might just nip out of the hole, nab the rabbit and drag it back under. This is annoying, and means you have to dig yet again. Do not put dead rabbits in a heap, as it causes the meat to bruise and spoil; instead lie them down singly, and when there is a lull in the excitement, you can drain them, hock them and hang them on a tree or fence to cool. When the day has finished, I will show you how to clean the catch and prepare it for cooking.

Now that you know what ferreters do, let us look at everything in detail, starting with choosing your ferret.

Chapter Two

Choosing your Ferrets

Good ferrets have been bought from markets and pet shops, but so have bad ferrets. By 'bad', I mean undernourished, sickly or fearful animals, neither well cared for nor well handled. Shorten the odds by buying from someone whose stock is clean, properly fed, well handled and well socialised to humans. Most areas have a ferret club which can put you in touch with responsible ferret breeders, and country shows are a good place to find them. Avoid people who bring kits (baby ferrets) for sale on the day, as anyone who subjects them to such a stressful day away from familiar surroundings, and possibly in the heat of the sun, is not a caring ferret-keeper. Healthy kits are much more likely to come via an organisation that takes your details and then puts you in touch with someone who has a litter. Before you go to see them – and baby ferrets are enchanting – have some idea of what you want. A ferret's average life span is seven or eight years, and some have reached their teens, so you are going to be together for a long time. Of course, there is no reason why you should not buy an adult ferret, which means that you can start ferreting right away without having to wait for it to grow up. Many ferret clubs do ferret rescue, and have an assortment of suitable animals that they will carefully place with the right sort of home. As I write, five of our ferrets are 'rescues' and every one is a good worker.

Much has been made of the recent interest in ferrets as show and pet animals, and some old-style ferreters will tell you that, to be any good, your ferret must come from working stock. I am happy to assure you that this is nonsense; unlike some breeds of dog, the working instinct has not been bred out of the show/pet ferret, and I own two from this stock myself which are superb workers. We ferreters have a lot for which to thank the show fraternity, for it is they who have improved the general health of the ferret by feeding and housing them properly, and by taking sick animals to the vet, thus interesting the veterinary profession in ferret ailments and treatment. Prior to this, sick ferrets were more often than not knocked on the head. Of course you can also get first-class, healthy ferrets from working homes, as the best will be every bit as well cared for, but if you lose your heart to a show-bred ferret, then go ahead and buy it; it will have been well reared, and the working instinct, believe me, is all there. Show ferrets also come in some lovely colours, and while it is true that a ferret does not bolt rabbits with the colour of its fur, you might as well get one that you like.

On the subject of colour, do not be confused by talk of 'polecats' and 'ferrets'. Ferrets are domestic animals which are closely related to the northern European polecat, rather as the dog is closely related to the wolf. Polecats and ferrets can interbreed and produce fertile offspring, as can dogs and wolves. The cross is not for the fainthearted (nor is the wolf/dog hybrid) and very few exist; they are simply a novelty

that some ferreters have tried. The cross will not do anything that a purebred ferret cannot, but they are very sharp
and quick, and of course beautifully marked with polecat
mask and colouring.

There are, however, many polecat-coloured ferrets which
are sometimes called polecats, and if you were to let it be
known that you were after a genuine polecat/ferret hybrid
you would soon be knee deep in them. Unscrupulous
ferreters (alas! they do exist) would try to offload many onto
you. A ferret of any colour is a ferret, but some people call
an albino ferret a ferret and a polecat-coloured ferret a polecat. This is why you may see advertisements for 'polecat x
ferrets', or 'ferret kits for sale – polecats and ferrets'. Some
breeders will even insist that the polecat-coloured members of
the same litter are real polecats, and the white ones are
ferrets! Do not be fooled – all of these are ferrets, whatever
the colour.

Ferrets can also be 'sandy' (brown and cream, which can
be any shade from chocolate to ginger), 'silvermitt' (polecat-
coloured with white feet), 'pastel polecat' (with polecat
markings in a paler shade of brown), 'silver' (white with dark
guard hairs and very dark red eyes), and 'coloured' (all the
in-between colours, some of which are quite spectacular). No
colour is better than any other, but some people prefer white
ferrets, especially if they are working with guns or hawks, as
the whites show up well and are never in danger from being
mistaken for something else.

The next decision is between male (hob or dog) or female
(jill or bitch) ferrets. This choice is personal to you, rather as
some people prefer dogs or horses of one sex, although the
circumstances in which you intend to keep and work your
ferrets can have some bearing on your decision. Jills tend to
be smaller than hobs, although we have one tiny hob which is
smaller than our smallest jill! A small ferret wearing a locator
collar can pass through the mesh of a purse net without dis-
turbing it unduly. Moreover some people will argue that a

large ferret will be more prone to killing underground, whereas a smaller one will tend to bolt the rabbits. For every theory there is a counter-theory; however, I will say that very large ferrets can be a penance if you are using purse nets, as they pull them around. If you are shooting or hawking over your ferret, or using a long net, a larger ferret will be fine, as long as it is not so big that it has trouble getting down the rabbit holes. One of my fellow ferreters likes to work big hobs that will hold a rabbit underground while he digs down to it. Large and strong, he gets a good haul of rabbits working this way, but as you may already have gathered, digging is not for me, and I prefer my rabbits to bolt.

The other consideration when deciding the gender of your ferrets is that you can keep any number of females together, but entire males will fight viciously with each other. Entire males and females equals babies, and you do not want those yet, if ever, but castrated males will live happily with females and other castrated males once the hormone levels have settled down after the operation, which can take some time. Castrated males work just as well as any other ferrets, and if, like me, you work your ferrets all year round, you will find them easier than entires, whose minds tend to be on other things during the breeding season, and who can get sulky and difficult if not allowed to mate. I would suggest that you start your ferreting career with two medium-sized jills or two smallish castrated hobs, and when you have a season's ferreting under your belt, you can add more if you wish, although you can work a hard season with only two ferrets.

If you have a vasectomised hob to bring your jills out of season (much the best way) remember that his instincts and desires are those of the entire hob, and he will fight any males and mate any females that he comes across during the breeding season. The only difference is that he 'fires blanks'. He does not know that, however, so treat him in every way as you would an entire hob.

*How big do you like your ferrets? These two are
exceptionally well-grown female kits aged four months.*

Ferrets are very playful, inquisitive creatures.

Choosing your kits from the beguiling little things in the litter is just like choosing a puppy or kitten: you want a lively, healthy animal with clean eyes, nose and coat, with feet and tail free from deformity. All baby animals nip and some ferrets go through a real vampire stage – my white jill was named *Venom* by her breeder, and she certainly lived up to her name, but she is a delight to handle now. Some kits nip more than others, but it is only a phase, and the more you handle them, the quicker they will get over it. Make real pets of your ferrets, for it will pay dividends when you start to work them. While you are waiting for them to grow up, you can start to accumulate some of the fascinating bits and pieces that make up a ferreter's working equipment.

Chapter Three

Ferreting Equipment

If you were to ask people who were ferreting before the introduction of myxomatosis in the early 1950s, they would assure you that all they took was a ferret in one pocket and a couple of nets in another, and maybe a 'big, mean old liner' (this last refers to a line ferret, and we will discuss its use later in this chapter). But if you were to try ferreting now using the methods they describe, you would be lucky to catch anything at all, partly because there is a bit more to it, and partly because times and the rabbit population have changed. The buries are forty years older and correspondingly larger; agriculture is different, the rabbit population is subject to extreme fluctuation due to the myxomatosis, and ferreters are probably much fonder of their ferrets than people were then. There is a lot of equipment needed for ferreting nowadays, unless you live in a remote and rabbit-infested area, and although costs are low compared to other sports, there is no point in wasting your money by purchasing the wrong kit. What suits one person will not always suit another, so if you can, go ferreting with a few different people so that you can try a wide variety of equipment, and buy cautiously until you have field-tested enough gear to know what you need.

Purse nets. Left: heavyweight hemp – a beautiful quality homemade net. Centre: shop-bought hemp in a lighter weight. Right: nylon net.

Purse nets for example come in hemp or nylon, several colours, and more mesh sizes than you can imagine. You can never have too many of these, and I have a friend who gives me handmade purse nets at every birthday and Christmas! Hemp is more expensive than nylon, heavier, and less hard-wearing, and unless you take care to hang up your hemp nets and dry them thoroughly after each use, they will rot, and after a few years the fibres will start to become brittle and break up anyway. Some ferreters 'pickle' their hemp nets in heathen brews of secret ingredients, but the nets then become stiff and difficult to handle, and the whole joy of the hemp net is its ease of use. Nylon is cheaper, rot-proof, lighter to carry, needs no care or maintenance – and tangles like blazes. There is a definite knack to handling nylon, and I do not have it. Heavier-gauge nylon is easier to work with, but means you will either have to make your own nets or find someone else to do it for you; only the very flimsy nylon nets may be bought over the counter.

Dry your nets thoroughly after each ferreting trip.

Long and dreary correspondence takes place in the sporting press about the mesh size of purse nets. The basics are that if the mesh is too big, small rabbits will escape, and if it is too small, ferrets will become tangled in the net because they cannot slip through easily. A ferret wearing a locator collar is wider than one without, and big ferrets obviously need bigger mesh than little ones. If you ferret with the help of a dog, it can

You need a wide enough mesh for the ferret to slip through with ease.

peg rabbits that slip the net so that they do not escape. It is more important for the ferret to be able to pass through the nets than for every small rabbit to be caught, and it means less work for you as well as less disturbance to the bury if you are not constantly having to reset disarranged nets. Manufactured nets tend to come in about 2-inch mesh size, which is quite adequate and functional.

Some ferreters take care to match the colour of the net to its surroundings – green nets in grass, brown in ditches, white in snow; others think that blue is appropriate because the rabbit will think that the net is part of the sky. Do not worry about any of that.The rabbit is in darkness, and the mouth of its hole appears to it in bright light. It cannot see your net, nor is it looking for it. If it leaves the bury at a gallop, the first it will know of the net is when it purses round him. If it is the 'hop cautiously and look' type, it will touch the net with its nose no matter what colour you are using.

Nets need pegs, which were traditionally hewn out of sharpened hazel sticks with a cleft cut in one side to hold the drawstring. These are a nuisance, as drawstring and peg have a tendency to part company. One can buy ready-made wooden pegs quite cheaply, and these have a hole so that you can feed the drawstring through and then knot it. If you paint the tops of these pegs a bright colour (I use fluorescent orange), you will be able to see them easily when you pick up your nets, and so reduce the chance of leaving nets behind, which apart from being expensive, will not endear you to the farmer. Pegs are also available in plastic, which is lighter than wood and lasts longer, but is not so easy to drive into hard ground. Some people use metal pegs, such as tent pegs, which will go into ground that nothing else will penetrate. There is a weight penalty here, but otherwise they are very good indeed.

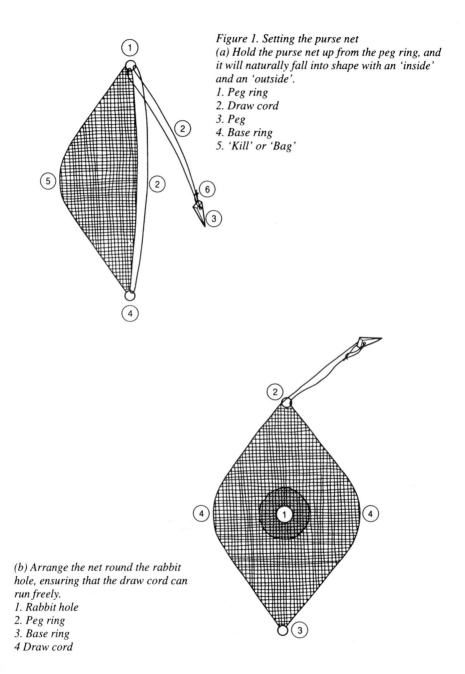

Figure 1. Setting the purse net
(a) Hold the purse net up from the peg ring, and it will naturally fall into shape with an 'inside' and an 'outside'.
1. Peg ring
2. Draw cord
3. Peg
4. Base ring
5. 'Kill' or 'Bag'

(b) Arrange the net round the rabbit hole, ensuring that the draw cord can run freely.
1. Rabbit hole
2. Peg ring
3. Base ring
4 Draw cord

16

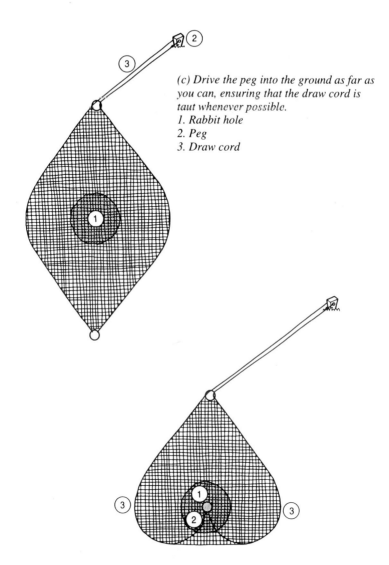

(c) Drive the peg into the ground as far as you can, ensuring that the draw cord is taut whenever possible.
1. Rabbit hole
2. Peg
3. Draw cord

(d) Flick the base ring and the bottom of the net right into the rabbit hole, so that the rabbit will tread on the net as it hits the 'kill'.
1. Rabbit hole
2. Base ring and bottom of net
3. Plenty of 'kill'

Getting a lively rabbit out of a purse net.

When setting your purse net, the entrance to the rabbit hole should be clear of clinging vegetation that will otherwise hamper the pursing action of the net. The rabbit will bolt out of the hole, not out of the earth, so spread the net over the hole with the peg ring uppermost. Then sink the peg in firmly as far away as the drawstring will allow. This means that the pursing action will commence as soon as the rabbit's weight hits the net. Next, take the bottom ring of the net and flick it into the rabbit hole so that the metal ring and about a quarter of the net lies on the tunnel floor. This again aids the pursing action, as the rabbit will tread on the net at the same time as it hits it with his head and body. Finally, open out the sides of the net so that the sides of the rabbit hole are covered. If the sides of the net slip down, pin them with tiny pieces of twig or pebble that will give way as soon as rabbit tumbles into the net. It is worth taking time and care over the setting of purse nets, especially in ensuring that the drawstring will run freely, and the peg will not pull out. Pegs may be tied to tree roots where they cannot easily be driven into the ground, but do not make the knot so fancy that you cannot free it with a kicking buck rabbit in your net!

Getting a rabbit out of a purse net while kneeling on the rabbit hole to prevent another bolt.

Nets may be folded around their pegs, rolled up and secured with elastic bands or clipped onto a rope which may be hung from a branch. Everyone works out their own way of carrying their nets, which need to be tangle- and debris-free before they are put away for the next time. I carry mine in a bright white rucksack, my only departure from dull colours in fieldwork, as I have found that a running rabbit will veer away from the strange object. If the bury exits are a short way from cover, I will put the rucksack right by the cover, which is sometimes enough to make the bolting rabbit go the long way round, and give the dog more chance of catching it.

A stop net crossing a ditch. Rabbits will bolt along a ditch if they can.

Stop nets and long nets can be used instead of or as a back-up to purse nets. A long net can be 100 yards long; stop nets are between 25 and 50 yards long. They can be used to bisect hedges or large buries, or to surround very thick cover to stop the rabbits that will try to bolt from one patch of cover to another. When set, the net is approximately 3 feet high, taut along the top, and with plenty of sag or 'kill' along the bottom. Modern electric fencing poles with a sharp metal spike at the bottom make better stakes than the traditional hazel, and the net is staked approximately every 5 feet. There are a few very good solo stop netters about, but two or three people can work the net much more easily than one.

Setting a long net.

These nets save time in setting, and you don't have to clear the buries of undergrowth, but they are a penance to use where there is loose debris, as they will pick up every thorn and branchlet. Where stop nets are good, they are very good, but they do require a particular type of terrain. Rabbits do not always run where one would like them to, and there are times when you will lose rabbits using a stop net that you would have caught with purse nets. The 100 yard long net is a little too much for most ferreting jobs unless you have several helpers; it really comes into its own when used across a field on a dark, windy night; this does not involve ferrets and is outside the scope of this book.

A stop net covering a difficult place.

A ferret working to the stop net.

A rabbit hitting a stop net at speed.

The rabbit tangled in the net, showing the necessity for plenty of 'kill' in the bottom of the net.

23

It requires skill to get a tangled rabbit out.

Probably the most expensive item for your ferreting will be the locator collars and box. The ferret locator collars, slim leather strips, come in two depth readings: 8 feet and 15 feet. Which one you choose will depend on the land you will be working. You may say that you have no intention of digging down to 15 feet, but if you are working steep banks, the tunnels can go down rapidly, and it is very irritating when a ferret goes beyond the range of the locator. Even if one is not digging, it is useful to know where the ferret is, and whether she is still or moving. Accuracy is variable below 8 feet, and these tiny transmitters can give false readings, particularly near metal or in damp conditions. I know of one area where there is sandy soil, and the presence of ironstone can affect the readings, but

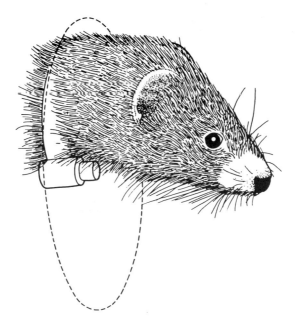

Figure 2. The locator correctly fitted under the ferret's neck. The dotted line shows the elliptical shape of the signal.

despite the frustration when the kit malfunctions, I would never put a ferret to ground without it. The collar should always be leather, which will stretch or break if the ferret gets it caught on a root underground, enabling her to wriggle free. She wears the collar with the transmitter under her throat, and the signal goes upwards and downwards in an elliptical shape. Always use the correct batteries; some people try to save money by using hearing-aid batteries, but they do not do the job and it is a false economy.

At the moment, the receivers are manufactured in a drab shade of grey, so I recommend that you wind some brightly coloured tape around yours to make it more visible. If you have the sort where the back is held on by screws, remember to take a screwdriver as well as a spare battery for the receiver, and of course, spare collar batteries. Some people tape over the battery housing on the collars before a day's use, which is a good system, as they are easily lost and spares are expensive. When you are digging to your ferret, it is depressingly easy to bury your receiver, so be careful!

Ferret locators.
Left: 8 foot collar.
Top: 15 foot collar,
with receiver box
below.

Fitting the collar.

Digging is generally done with an implement called a graft, or you may prefer to dig with an ordinary garden spade. Some people like to keep the blade of the graft sharpened in order to strike through tree roots, and a trowel is useful in tight places. There are lightweight folding grafts available, which are very convenient for friable soils but not good enough for clay or chalk, so pick the tool for the job. Digging out a lying-up ferret is not like digging the garden; there is a certain knack to it.

Using the locator – a 'fix' has been found, and it is time to dig.

Having found the place from which the transmitter signal is coming most strongly, put the receiver down over it so that you can hear if the ferret starts to move. Some ferrets will move on as soon as digging commences, and indeed may be persuaded to shift if you slap the flat of the graft on the ground a few times. Any hole you dig must be backfilled to the best of your ability. Of course you will not have enough earth, because you will be digging out a tunnel which you will be filling in solidly. The first sod of earth out is the last one back in, and should be as big as possible to provide a good 'plug'. So dig round in a circle and carefully lift out a good big chunk of earth. Check repeatedly with the receiver as you dig, and be careful when you get near to your ferret because you do not want to slice into her with the graft.

An experienced ferret will be very trusting when dug to. The rabbit is the other side of the graft.

Once you break through into the tunnel, pull out the earth carefully with your hands or the trowel until you can see what is going on. Your ferret may be very excited, or, if it is the first time she has been dug to, she may be nervous. She may have killed her rabbit, or it may be alive and very cross. A high-velocity smack in the face from a rabbit hurts even more than a petulant nip from a ferret, so get hold of the rabbit firmly and pull it out. Once you have despatched it, check the tunnel at both ends in case your ferret has shepherded a line of rabbits into a stop for you – my own record is eight rabbits out of one stop. Having put all the rabbits to one side and given the ferret a drink before popping her back into her box, replace all the earth, top it with the big first cut and tread it down as neatly as possible. You will not be popular if a farm animal steps into a hole that you have left and damages itself, so leave the area as safe as you can make it.

Always backfill any digging as neatly as you can.

29

Sometimes it may be impossible to dig, and if the ferret stays below, you must try to get her out by other means. You have a legal as well as a moral responsibility to do so; ferrets are domestic animals, and it is an offence to release or abandon them. The ferret is also an accomplished killer of poultry, and will soon make her presence felt in the farmyard. Therefore you must do everything possible to get her back.

If the signal is still, an accident may have befallen her, she may have taken off her collar or she may be asleep. If slapping the graft on the ground, or starting to dig as close as you can to where you believe her to be does not make her move, try calling or whistling at the nearest bury entrance. If you have a rabbit, paunch it and leave it at the rabbit hole, but either secure or keep hold of it to prevent her dragging it back underground. If that does not work, leave her carry box at the mouth of the rabbit hole, and if possible, put a morsel of rabbit kidney or liver in it. An alternative is to dig a deep vertical shaft with the rabbit bait at the bottom. This will lure the ferret in but not allow her out. Remember, however, that ferrets can jump and climb so it needs to be a very deep hole, which is inadvisable in a livestock field.

A deep hole is necessary for a ferret trap. Note the traditional shape of the graft.

If you have to leave your ferret, return as early as possible the following day. If she is unhurt, she will most likely be asleep in her carrying box. If you cannot find her, keep coming back and leaving fresh bait, for although some ferrets adapt to feral living, most do not and the ferret rescue societies take in many very sick ferrets that have been accidentally lost or even deliberately abandoned.

Three carrying boxes. Left: lightweight plywood built by Elspeth Rodwell of the GEM Ferret Care Group.

Double ferret box curved to fit the waist, built by Tony Minett of the Surrey Working Lurcher Club.

When you are digging to your ferret, remember that it is not only rabbits that live down rabbit holes, and mind your hands. I remember a friend pulling out a fat rat, and the panic that followed, as both he and his dog were terrified of rats, as were the other two ferreters. I am afraid all I could do was laugh. The rat escaped unharmed.

You will need a carrying box for your ferrets. Some people use a stout bag or sack, but this is not comfortable for the ferrets, which can get cold and wet. There is also the very real danger of someone accidentally stepping on the bag. If the box is very light, it will be easier to carry; if it is stronger, you will be able to sit on it. Being short, I find two small boxes easier to carry than one big one, and if your box can be compartmentalised, you will find it easier to get out the ferret you want without the rest boiling over and trying to join in. I have seen home-made boxes which are curved to sit better round the waist, and boxes which can be carried like rucksacks. The broader the carrying strap, the more comfortable the box will be for you, and the ideal box has an easily adjusted strap so that people of different sizes can easily carry it.

The disadvantage of a box, apart from its weight, is the noise that the ferrets will make scrabbling to come out and play. Apart from that, it is a very safe and comfortable conveyance for your ferrets. Make sure that it can be opened and fastened with one hand, as your other is likely to be full of ferret, and ensure that the lid is not the sort that could snap down and crush the ferrets if they try to get out. A ferret's ambition is always to be somewhere else, so check your box often and make sure that it is still ferret-proof. Plenty of air-holes or a grille will provide ventilation, and go easy on the bedding, as the ferrets tend to block up the air holes with it. I use shredded newspaper, but hay, straw or shavings are just as good. Metal boxes should not be used, as they are cold in the winter and hot in the summer, and produce condensation. If I am working on a warm day, I carry my ferrets in a wire cat-carrier, which means they stay cooler. I then change them to more conventional transport when we leave the car. A spare ferret box is always useful, either to leave behind should you lose a ferret, or to convey an extra ferret home should you find one – and from time to time you will!

It is not wise to kennel a strange ferret with your own: ferrets are territorial, and you could end up with a fight. The new ferret may also be incubating a disease, or could be very run down. So take her home separately, and keep her separate while you remove her ticks and bring her back to health. If you do not want to keep her, there are branches of ferret rescue societies in most areas, and they are very good at rescue and rehabilitation. Larger animal rescue societies are sometimes alarmingly ignorant, and I know of people who have been told to release their foundling 'back to the wild'– which of course must not be done.

Your rabbiting arsenal will also include something to clear bramble – secateurs are marvellous for most jobs, protective gloves for use while clearing buries: something for your ferret to drink and something to drink it out of, because she will work up a thirst moving about underground, your permission, and some form of identification.

Now let us see what was used by the old-timers. Prior to the invention of the locator, a lain-up ferret would be found by using a line ferret. This would be a large, dominant hob, and he would be kept alone to encourage a surly temperament. When working, he would wear a collar with a very long length of line attached, and this line would be knotted at regular intervals so that as he went underground and the line was paid out, the handler would count the knots and know how far in he was. The line ferret would find the lain-up ferret and drive her off her kill, which he would then stay with and eat, while his handler dug down to him.

A fair amount of skill was involved in tracing the liner, as rabbit tunnels are not straight or level, and the line could easily foul on roots and stones underground. The noise of the hob driving off the jill might assist, and some dogs are very good at indicating where a ferret is underground. The ferreter might use a probe – a metal or wooden rod which would be inserted into the ground to feel the way of the tunnel, and which would carry vibration and sound up its shaft. It is not surprising that, with the use of the locator, this method of tracing a ferret underground is used by few people, although with experienced operators, it is most efficient. The locator takes a lot of the work out of finding a missing ferret, and of course there is no need for a hob ferret to be kept alone purely to do this job. On the other hand, locator equipment can fail, collars and battery caps can come off, but the line ferret will always find the jill and the kill. A modern variation is to work the jills uncollared, and for the liner to wear a transmitter instead of a line when he is needed. Take your choice, but if you get the chance to work with an old-fashioned liner and an experienced ferreter, take it, because it is a worthwhile skill to know.

Muzzling and coping are largely things of the past now, and rightly so. When people thought that a ferret had to be starved to make her work, she was muzzled to stop her killing, staying with the kill and feasting on it. The muzzles could be of string, metal or leather. Muzzling is still legal, but most unwise, as if the ferret meets something fierce underground, such as a rat or a mink, she will not be able to defend herself, and should she get lost, she would starve to death. In the old days, a ferret could be coped, i.e. have holes made in her mouth, which was then sewn shut, or have her teeth pulled out or broken off. These methods are now illegal, but still crop up from time to time. I was at a country show not long ago with one of my ferrets on my lap having her tummy tickled, and a spectator was convinced that I only dared to do this because 'she's had all her teeth pulled out, hasn't she?' She has not, and I gently lifted her lips to show him.

Some people like to use bells on their ferrets, although I have tried them and not found them very helpful. Underground, the bell quickly becomes fouled with earth, and it takes better ears than mine to hear a bell once a ferret is in a bury. Above ground, when working in thick undergrowth, the use of bells can be a little more successful, but I remain unenthusiastic, as there is usually enough ambient noise to drown the tiny rattle of the bell. One does not know how noisy the world is until one is listening for a ferret – the drone of traffic, even though the road may be miles away, the noise of farm machinery and live-stock, passing aircraft, even birdsong, is amazingly intrusive. I always seem to be near a particularly loud bird when I am waiting to hear a ferret. Try bells by all means, but be sure to fix them onto your ferret with something like a piece of shirring elastic, so that the ferret can easily escape if the bell becomes caught on something. You may lose a lot of bells, but that is better than losing a ferret.

Keepers of pet ferrets often use bells, especially when the ferret permanently has the run of the house or flat. Free-range ferrets are common as pets in Scandinavian countries and the USA especially – free-range within the house, that is, for they are no different from their hutch-kept cousins and would readily escape from a garden if they could. We are very lucky in Britain, for if we want to go ferreting and we have the landowner's permission, we can just go out with no further restriction. In some countries, however, such as Spain, ferreting is illegal, and if one examines the ferreting situation in North America, there is nowhere that the ordinary member of the public has unrestricted ferreting. In some states, ferrets may be kept as pets but not worked, in some they may only be worked by licensed pest controllers under stipulated circum-stances, and in others one needs the equivalent of the British dangerous wild animals licence even to keep one! In European countries, most pet ferrets are spayed or castrated, so kits are hard to come by and command a high price. How easy we have it here, where we can buy ferret kits cheaply and without restriction, and go ferreting whenever the fancy takes us.

Not long ago, I almost lost one of my most experienced ferrets, a jill that would never lay up. She went down a rabbit hole at ten past nine one Saturday morning, and did not

35

reappear. The locator could not find her. The warren, although only of average size, was adjacent some very big rabbit workings, and I was concerned that it might after all link up with them, and my ferret may have travelled far back into the hill. We were working chalk downland, nasty to dig at the best of times, and with the odd stunted tree clinging for its life to the hillside.

It is never wise to dig too soon, so my partner left me minding the bury while he went on to ferret the next one, and I waited for my jill to reappear. Presently, I started to get a signal from the locator, coming through the intertwined roots of the only two trees on the bury. We ran the other jill through, hoping that she would drive the first one to the surface, but she came out quickly with no success. We put a collar on the hob, and sent him down, but he was out just as fast. We paunched a rabbit and left it staked outside the hole nearest to where the signal was coming from, still with no result. The signal was steady at 4 feet, which could have meant that the ferret had slipped her collar and gone elsewhere, or that she was dead, injured or trapped. We tried desperately to dig, but were hampered by the tree roots as well as the remains of a fallen tree just below the ground surface. We were forced to abandon the dig at nightfall, leaving a ferret box behind which was baited with a rabbit liver.

That night it rained for the first time in many weeks, and when we went back at first light, the ground was treacherous. The ferret still had not returned, and the signal was steady at 4 feet, not having moved at all during the night. It did not look good.

Help arrived in the form of the gamekeeper whose beat we were on. He had driven up the hill as far as he could safely take the Land Rover, and we helped him to unload an arsenal of digging equipment that was way outside the scope of most ferreters! He was used to digging out terriers, and it showed. The dead tree that had given us so much trouble was dispersed with axe, a pick and an economy of effort that was astonishing to see. Shovelfuls of loose chalk and soil were removed, and then came the delicate job of working through the roots of the living trees without harming them. Next came solid chalk.

At exactly 4 feet, we heard scratching, and realised that the ferret, which had never been dug to in five years of working life, was digging towards the sounds of rescue. We carefully scooped out the chalk from around a root, and there she was, safe, uninjured, very thirsty, and very pleased to see us. She had been trapped by the body of a rabbit that she had killed, which had wedged her against the tree roots and chalk, leaving her with no way out except to eat her way through the body of the fallen rabbit. Luckily there had been enough air for her to survive. The tiny transmitter in her collar had been going for close on thirty hours, and had been absolutely accurate. There is no doubt that we would have been unable to rescue her without the locator, and it was not until the last few minutes that I realised we were not digging down to a dead ferret. A Land Rover, a pick, an axe and a gamekeeper may be outside the normal range of ferreting equipment, but I certainly recommend that you never put a ferret to ground, no matter how reliable, without a locator.

Chapter Four

Gaining Permission – and Keeping It!

Despite the fact that rabbits are a serious agricultural pest, gaining ferreting permission to hunt on other people's land can be very difficult at first. But, once you start to acquire permission land, the whole thing very soon snowballs, and within a couple of years you will be in a position to help other ferreters by introducing them to landowners who would like help in controlling their rabbits.

The first step is to join your local ferret club. They will have a list of landowners who welcome ferreters, and most established members will be pleased to have an extra pair of hands on a ferreting trip. Everybody works differently, and you will learn all sorts of methods of rabbiting. There is no right or wrong way; just try everything and reach your own conclusions. At first you may have to travel long distances to your hunting grounds, and cope with difficult, unproductive land, but just learn what you can.

Rabbit damage on the South Downs.

If there is no ferret club to help you with introductions, look around and see where the rabbit problems are locally. Remember, nobody likes a 'cold caller', and landowners are rightly suspicious of strangers. They may also have had ferreters on the land before who caused them trouble, so allow them to get to know you before you start asking them for favours. Keepered estates, farms, golf courses, hospitals, market gardens, allotments, private paddocks and gardens can all suffer rabbit damage, but nobody is going to give you *carte blanche* to go ferreting until they know that you are trustworthy. Chat to the person at the allotment, buy eggs at the farmhouse door, find out the name of the farmer or farm manager and see if casual help is needed from time to time, such as during haymaking. Some of my best rabbiting permission has been given by gamekeepers, but they have a hard job and meet all sorts of people, so they will not be falling over themselves to help you until they are sure that you are all right. Go with an introduction if you can; very occasionally it is possible to help for a season, beating etc., but availability varies from shoot to shoot, and a complete stranger is unlikely to be taken on unless someone can vouch for him or her. Following the local foxhounds, beagles or minkhounds on foot is a good way to meet country people and let them get to know you in their own time, and presently you may get the opening you need. Moreover if it takes country people a long time to trust you, it takes them no time at all to condemn you, so do not put a foot wrong. Keep to the footpaths, do not allow your dogs or children to be unruly on private land, do not park inconsiderately, and *never poach*. It will be neither forgiven nor forgotten, and will decisively end any chance you have to legitimate work with your ferrets.

Rabbit damage.

If you follow this advice, then when you ask for permission to ferret, it will be off someone who knows you by sight and quite possibly by name, who remembers the morning you helped the little boy who fell off his pony when it would not jump the ditch, and who knows that you keep to the footpaths and respect his crops and fences. I once had a morning out following hounds on foot, and a very posh gentleman and I were filling our pockets and hats with the wonderful mushrooms we found in one of the fields. Conversation turned to rabbits, and I ended up with a fair bit of permission as well as a couple of pounds of mushrooms!

More rabbit damage.

When you come to talk to a landowner about ferreting, dress tidily, arrive in a clean car, and leave your dogs and children at home. Make sure that you know the farm boundaries, and find out the neighbours' names, for boundary disputes are a way of life in the country. Never believe that neighbours will not mind if you cross the boundary onto their land while after rabbits, but approach them and find out for yourself. There may be many conditions to your new permission, such as not hunting on a Sunday or handing over the greater part of the catch, which after all does belong to the landowner. If the request is 'no dogs' then leave the dog at home, no matter how well trained it may be. After you have proved yourself reliable, these conditions may well change. I find that on average I tend to do a year's 'probation', after which the rules are relaxed and I can do pretty much as I please within the limits of good manners. When you have been ferreting one farm for a year or so, ask if you may have a reference, and then you can approach other locals. You will get a few refusals for every agreement but even a refusal can change if you leave it a while and then ask again another day.

Damage on the South Downs caused by rabbits.

Golf course managers can be very helpful to ferreters, but you will be very restricted. Golfers must not be upset, and they are sensitive souls. The hallowed turf must not be dug, so if your ferret lies up, you will be stuck waiting until she consents to come out. Only the most angelic dogs should be used and even the best trained dog has a knack of fouling the most obvious places. If yours does, clear it up. I once had a very exciting morning on a certain Scottish golf course during which my helpful lurcher assisted someone to find his lost ball.

The golfer was very pleased, which was just as well, as a few minutes later he was interrupted in mid-swing by a rabbit and a lurcher hurtling across his feet. The dog caught the rabbit and the golfer did not curse us, so we got away with it, but remember that it only needs one word to the management from an angry member and your services will be dispensed with.

The grounds of hospitals and nursing homes are often plagued with rabbits, but here you must be careful not to upset the patients, who may well have given them all names. The same applies to boarding schools, although you can, of course, work them in the holidays. You may even find the odd pupil wanting to help you, and those kids can be very helpful as they know the grounds inside out. Beware of one thing, however. Children do get 'crushes' on adults, and parents and guardians can misunderstand. So if you have a regular child helper, be sure that the family is happy and I would suggest that you do not allow him or her to get on first-name terms with you.

Private gardens and pony paddocks can be the easiest places to gain permission, and the most difficult to work. We will be looking at these in detail in a later chapter, but I would recommend that you start with the easier land, or take someone experienced along with you.

Having obtained your permission, make sure you keep it. Be seen to turn up regularly (I have often been given permission with the comment, 'we had someone else but he only came a couple of times') and if for any reason you give up working that particular farm introduce another reliable person to take your place if you can. Park your car out of the way, and pass the time of day briefly with the landowner if you see him. Apart from being polite, this gives him a chance to update you on any changes, such as the movement of livestock from one field to another, or fields he would like you to keep off for the time being. I have to confess to inadvertently poaching 50 acres or so for *six* years; the farmer had sold the land, and I had not realised! Luckily I found out before I was found out, and the farmer thought it was all very funny.

Listen to gossip but never carry it, and you will be well thought of. If on the way to the buries, you see livestock in trouble, or a fence down, do something about it and then tell the farmer straightaway – do not wait until you have finished ferreting. If you helped on the land before you asked for ferreting permission, do not stop when you have it. Try to avoid ferreting in fields with livestock in: horses gallop about, breaking legs and fences, sheep die for no particular reason, and abort lambs for even less reason, and bullocks are divinely curious, and will surround you, wreck your nets and terrorise your ferret. Backfill any digging that you do very firmly so that stock using that field are not at risk – a field that is empty now may have stock in it next week. Some people like every rabbit hole filled in before you leave so that they can see where you have been, and also which holes the rabbits open up·again. Dispose of paunch responsibly, burying it at a decent depth, not just in a token scrape in the ground. You will not be popular if the farm dogs find the paunch and eat it, only to bring it back up on the kitchen floor later. I know someone who lost permission from a very amiable farmer because his wife became so cross at having to clear up rabbit guts in the kitchen.

When you go home, paunch a brace of young rabbits and leave them by the farmhouse door. If you are invited in for a cup of tea and a slice of cake, so much the better.

A word about the law: even though rabbits are a problem 'trespassing in pursuit of coney' is a crime. The farmer may welcome you on his land, but the policeman who stops you a few miles down the road will not know that unless you can prove it. Make sure you get your permission in writing, something like this:

A. Farmer
Poverty Farm
Fallowlands
Blankshire
10 October 1995

To Whom It May Concern
Joe Ferreter has my permission to go ferreting for
rabbits on my land, and to remove the catch.

A. Farmer

Some farmers hate writing almost as much as they hate
filling in forms for the Ministry of Agriculture, so if it helps,
suggest that you write the permission on their headed
notepaper, and they sign it. Be precise: if you intend to hunt
other quarry by other means, or hunt by night as well as day,
ensure that it is specified on the permission, and be sure that it
says that you may remove the catch.

When you have your permission, photocopy it and keep the
original in a safe place. Keep one copy on you whenever you
go hunting, as well as some sort of personal identification. You
may also want to lodge another copy at the local police station;
there is no legal requirement to do this, nor is it necessary to
notify the police every time you go hunting, but in areas where
poaching is a problem, it can save time.

Be sure that the person who gives you permission is actually
authorised to do so. A tenant farmer may nominate someone
for pest control, without the agreement of the leasing
landowner, and it is better to steer clear of any conflict between
the two. If an estate owner gives you permission, it is a necessary courtesy to approach the gamekeeper and agree it with
him as well, for he will need to know who you are, where you
are and what you are doing. And if you are working land as
the guest of another ferreter, ascertain tactfully the extent of
his permission – I once narrowly avoided a very unpleasant

incident when it transpired that 'permission' had been given by the cowman, and the farmer knew nothing about it!

References are invaluable, especially if you move to a new district and have to start building permission up again from scratch. But nothing is better than people meeting you face to face and getting to know you, so get about and get known.

Chapter Five

Entering Your Ferrets to Quarry

Ferrets are natural hunters and enter to quarry with immense pleasure. However, a rabbit is by no means a helpless or defenceless creature, and to get the best out of your ferrets, it is wise to see things from the rabbit's point of view.

How soon can you start working your ferrets? If they are adults, you can start as soon as they come to you confidently and enjoy being handled. If they are kits which you have obtained in June or July, they should be ready to work at the turn of the year. They can and will work earlier, but they will tire more easily, they risk being hurt, and they may be put off the game completely. Let them grow up, and enjoy their kitten-hood with them; they are domestic animals and delight in the company of a caring human. Whenever you approach their quarters to feed or play with them, give the same whistle or call, and they will soon respond to it. Later, when they are in a bury or thick brambles, you will be able to call them to you with the same sound. It will not work every time, but they will certainly respond often enough, and it will be a great help to you. Make sure that your ferrets are used to the sight of feet; many only see their owners from the chest up to start with, and when they are put on the ground to hunt, they find themselves surrounded by great big feet that they have never come across before. Accustom them to wearing a locator collar, first without and then with batteries. The collar weighs little to us, but it is quite heavy for a ferret, and they will not like it at first. Later, when they realise that putting the collar on means going out to play, they will chuckle and bounce with delight when they see it. It does not make getting it on any easier, but at least their wriggles are wriggles of pleasure. Some people find that giving their ferrets something to eat or drink makes putting the collar on much easier, but I am afraid it does not work with mine – they are far too excited at the prospect of going ferreting to calm down and eat anything.

Collared up and ready to go.

There are people who construct artificial buries with drain-pipes, and 'train' their ferrets to enter these. That is fine if you want to do it, and it is a great source of amusement to the ferrets, but it is not necessary, as ferrets are already programmed to go down holes. You may even hear of elaborate 'training' involving putting a ferret on a line and letting it enter a rabbit hole for a few feet before dragging it out. Do not bother with this; the reality is far easier on both of you.

You need a small rabbit bury, and plenty of time. Do not worry about catching rabbits at first; the session is for the ferret. Remember that she will be rather excited and perhaps a little upset from being jolted about in her carrying box, so when you take her out, give her a tiny titbit and make a fuss of her. Then place her by the entrance of a rabbit hole, and wait.

The chances are that she will take a few steps down, fluff up her tail and back out, possibly to run up your leg for comfort! So comfort her, pet her and talk to her, then put her back down. Presently, she will be brave enough to go right down the hole. Some ferrets will run down to ground the first time, some agonise at the entrance to the hole for several visits. Do not interfere, and never force the issue. Remember that the ferret is still young and give her time – quite the best working ferret in my present team was very slow to enter. If you have the ferret's mother or another adult that she is used to, let the adult go down the hole, and the young one will follow her. Do not, whatever you do, try it with a ferret she has never met before, as there could well be a fight, and the kit might then be too frightened to come back to you.

Left: a very excited small polecat hob with tail fizzed out. Compare his size with the jills in the photograph on page 9.

After she has gone underground, rabbits may or may not bolt, chiefly depending on whether or not there are any in the bury, and your ferret may stay down for quite some time as she follows the delicious scents. She may also shoot out of the bury, and bounce round you, chattering away to let you know what fun it all is. There are some sad souls who get rid of a ferret if she dares to play at the bury entrance when she should be 'working'! But as far as I am concerned she should be allowed to enjoy herself. Nothing is 'work' to a ferret: they are happy little things who really enjoy going down holes and hunting for rabbits. The experience is very new for her, and if she comes out full of excitement and wants to tell you about it, why stop her? Soon enough she will want to go down the hole again and have some more fun, and this time it will be with much more confidence. When she comes out next, let her get clear of the rabbit hole, call her with the special whistle or sound that you use, gently take her up, make a fuss of her and give her a titbit. Then take her home. The first trip is very tiring for a novice ferret, and you do not want her to curl up and have a good sleep underground.

An equally excited silver jill leaping at her rabbit.

A few ferrets lurk in the rabbit hole entrance and will not come out after they have been underground for the first time, although this is rarely a problem if they have been well handled. If this happens with one of yours, do not rush her, but leave her carrying box open by the rabbit hole, with a small titbit inside, like a piece of liver. She will come out in her own good time (which is why you never start a training session when you are pressed for time) and when she does, do not snatch her up as soon as you can get hold of her. Let her come right out. She might climb into her box or onto your lap, or she might dart back underground again. Let her. Eventually she will come out and come to you, but if you snatch at her at this stage, you will turn her into a 'skulker' – that infuriating animal that refuses to come out of a bury but peeps out just out of reach down a hole. Skulkers can be cured with time, patience and gentle handling, but it is better not to frighten them into the habit in the first place.

If you are working with a confirmed skulker, remember that they get thirsty underground and place a heavy dish of milk and water a ferret length out of the bury. It will not be able to drag the dish back underground, so it will have to come out properly to drink. Another useful emergency tactic is to wriggle a paunched rabbit at the hole where your skulker last put in an appearance, let her grab hold of it and draw her out. I ferreted half a winter with such a ferret, a super working ferret in every way except that rough handling by a previous owner had made him a skulker. He would come to the bury entrance after everything had been bolted, I would rabbit him out and off we would go to the next bury. Eventually he started coming to hand of his own accord, and has never skulked again; it was just a matter of building up his confidence. Do not have any truck with so-called 'cures' for skulking that involve force; by far the best and most permanent way is to understand that the ferret would like to come out, but is frightened to, and to revive her trust in being handled. Ferrets are very small compared to us, and a snatching hand can easily make them fearful.

Sometimes ferrets that normally come straight to hand will appear at the bury entrance and not come out: this does not mean that they have suddenly become skulkers; they are simply asking you for help. There may be something down there that is not a rabbit, or there may be a rabbit, but out of reach. I know of one occasion where a reliable ferret came several times to a bury entrance and then went down and stayed down. On being dug to, we found three rabbits up on a shelf that she was too small to get to. Another time, an exasperated hob ferret, having failed to communicate his problem to his owner, dragged a very sick female ferret out of the bury. She was starving, dehydrated, covered in ticks and ready to die, but she made a full recovery and still lives with her rescuer.

All sorts of things other than rabbits live down rabbit holes: snakes, little owls, rats, cats, foxes, stoats, and even the odd pheasant, have all been bolted by ferrets. If your ferret ever refuses to enter a hole, especially if she fluffs up and hisses, do not force her. She knows what is there and you do not, so take her away and try somewhere else. And do not stick your hand down the hole, either!

After your ferret has started entering rabbit holes freely and with confidence, and is coming back to you quite happily, start putting purse nets over the holes to get her used to passing through the mesh. Now you can take her ferreting in earnest, but do be very careful the first few times you dig down to her. Like terriers, ferrets soon learn that the sound of the graft means that help is on the way, but like terriers, some find it frightening the first few times.

Even the tamest ferret can become very fired up when working, so if your ferret emerges from the bury very excited do not touch her until she has calmed down. Once the tail is back to its normal size, offer her the back of your hand to sniff and then pick her up. A dab of saliva on the back of the hand also has a calming influence, for the ferret will stop and smell it, lick it perhaps, and settle down.

The ferret's motives when hunting are very different from ours. We want her to bolt the rabbits; she wants to kill them. If she is in a position to kill, then she will do so, but if she is not hungry, she will leave the carcase at once and carry on hunting. She may become trapped behind it, in which case she will have to eat her way out, so when the locator shows that she is still for ten minutes or so, dig down to her. Otherwise she will bolt what she can and kill what she can, and when she has cleared the bury, she will come out to tell you that she has finished. Our ferrets will clear a bury and move on to the next one if we let them, or come up to us if they are getting tired. Tiredness is the second most common cause of lie-up after hunger, so keep an eye on your ferret, and give her a drink and time for a sleep if she shows signs of weariness. Although we call ferreting work, to her it is not work but fun, and when it stops being fun, she will stop doing it.

If your ferret has had a hard time trying to bolt a rabbit, take her up and let her rest – use another one for the remainder of the day, or go home. An angry rabbit can give a ferret a tremendous kicking, and you will hear the thumping quite clearly as you stand by the bury. If your ferret comes out looking a bit groggy, check her over and let her rest. Ferrets are tough and full of spirit, but they can and do become injured on occasion, so be aware.

Although this book is concerned with working ferrets to rabbits, a few words are appropriate here about their other main quarry, the rat. A lot of ferreters, myself included, only use their ferrets on rabbits, but it is worth remembering that after the first great myxomatosis plagues in the 1950s virtually made the rabbiting ferret redundant, it was the rat hunters who kept the population going, ironically along with the fur trade and the laboratories. Show ferrets were unknown then, and although the occasional working ferret was treated well enough to be called a pet, most were not, and purely pet ferrets were almost unknown.

Ferrets are used to bolt rats which, once out in the open, can be killed using dogs, sticks or occasionally, guns. Dogs, preferably terriers, although almost anything will rat – are best; one's reflexes have to be fast to kill a rat with a stick (although in days gone by, some people were famed for catching rats by hand!) and even faster to shoot them. Rat hunting with ferrets means fast action, often in dim light, and many people prefer a white ferret for this job so that it is not accidentally killed. Jill ferrets are most often used for ratting, because they are smaller. A small hob would be every bit as useful, but they are not so easy to find. There are accounts of small, fast, very sharp ferrets, called 'greyhound ferrets', which were used for ratting in the past, but they have since probably died out. They may have existed as a strain or they may be the stuff of old ratters' tales. You will hear a lot about them, and may even meet people who claim to have known someone who bred them, but they do not seem to exist today, so ratting ferreters make use of small jills.

If you compare the size of a rat with that of a small jill, then you will have some idea of the task that is involved in rat hunting. Whereas young rats that are still greycoats, and most adult bucks, will bolt easily, a doe rat is a different matter entirely. With or without young – and a doe rat is pregnant, nursing or both from a very early age – she is a wicked adversary, and can inflict a lot of damage to a ferret. Because rats harbour so much disease, their bites fester if untreated, and you risk infection from handling a ferret that has been ratting. Ferrets do not get Weil's disease (leptospirosis), which is spread by contact with rat urine, but humans do. It used to be called 'rat catcher's yellows', from the jaundiced colour of the skin in infected people. So be very particular about washing and disinfecting your hands after you have been ratting, and I strongly recommend that you do not take sandwiches!

It is an unusual ferret that will rat hunt for many seasons

(although some do) because of the viciousness of the quarry. Do not, therefore, start your ferret on rats until she has had at least one, and preferably two, seasons of rabbit work. When she finally gives up on rats, respect her wishes and return her to rabbiting. Never try to force her to continue rat work once she has decided that she has had enough.

Many people consider ratting the finest sport of all, and of course somebody has to do it, but if that is what you choose, be very careful with your ferrets' health and your own, and never skimp on hygiene.

Chapter Six

The Lie of The Land

Rabbits are past masters at survival and build their homes with this in mind. A rabbit bury is a masterpiece of escape holes, shelved tunnels, vertical shafts, blind stops (dead ends) and natural obstacles such as tree roots, all of which help the rabbit to elude a pursuer. It extends downwards and outwards much further than you might believe, until you have to use your locator or notice your dog marking a tiny hole some distance away that you have not seen and would not have recognised as a rabbit hole if you had. You will develop an instinct for these 'pop holes' as you become more experienced, but a dog is quicker! As well as these emergency exits, there are tunnels which extend almost to the surface, out of which rabbits will dig their way if pressed, and the first that you will know about them will be the shower of earth and dead leaves as the rabbit erupts to safety.

*A ferret confidently working
a big bury with her owner.*

You will be told that the best buries to ferret are the 'two-holers' in the middle of a field. These do exist, but they are extremely uncommon, for the simple reason that they are a lot less safe than buries that are well dug into a hedgerow, bramble patch or fence line. You will see hillside buries where the digging extends downwards and inwards further than you would ever want to attempt to send your ferret. There are sand-dune buries where your ferret will tire quickly as she tries to dig through falling sand; clay soil buries that will break your heart if not your graft, and buries that were once rubbish tips – a fact that you will discover too late, when you are unable to dig at all through the mess of broken glass and scrap metal which lies just beneath the surface. These are perfect for rabbits but not good for ferrets, so leave them alone.

Figure 3. A small bury.
A. Pop holes some distance from the main bury.
B. Stop ends or blind stops.
C. Emergency exits which do not quite reach to the surface, but which can be excavated in seconds by a rabbit. These weak ground areas, sometimes called 'strikes', are very dangerous to livestock.

A ferret emerging from a hidden pop hole.

There is an Army saying that 'time spent in reconnaissance is never wasted'. Get to know your land and every bury on it, even if some of them are impossible or unwise for you to ferret. Rabbits are much more mobile than most people suppose, and will leave a bury *en masse* for a variety of reasons. You may arrive at a site one day to find all the rabbits gone, although two weeks previously the place may have been teeming with them. Since then, there may have been prolonged heavy rain, or contractors may have been in with heavy machinery or agrochemicals, or they may have moved for some other reason. It makes sense therefore, and is good woodcraft, to walk your permission land regularly and see where the rabbits are and where they run to when they are disturbed. Do not be swayed by reports of 'hundreds of rabbits all over the place'; go and see for yourself where they play, where they feed and where they live, because you can only ferret them out of the place where they sleep. Note the buries that you can work, and bear in mind that even a small bury can use up over thirty purse nets quite easily.

When you choose your bury, ask yourself where the rabbits are likely to run to. There may be well-worn paths that they have made or tunnels through undergrowth, or you may have to use your common sense and think about the surrounding cover and what refuge it offers a dispossessed rabbit. A hedgerow rabbit will not run across an open field if it can run up or down the hedgerow and find a safe haven further on. A rabbit will not necessarily leave from the hole nearest its destination, but may choose one with the thickest cover and then turn at speed to catch its enemies flatfooted as it races for another hole. If you are netting buries close by each other, it is a good idea to net all of them before you start to ferret. Then if a rabbit escapes you and runs to the next bury, there is every chance that it will 'backnet' itself in a net that you have already set. You will need to put the pegs in as deeply as you can; the rabbit will be very determined to get down the hole, and will not be easy to haul out. If you do not react quickly you run the risk of losing both the rabbit and the net.

A lovely wood, almost clear of undergrowth, perfect for purse netting.

If a rabbit has been bolted once, and has managed to get to safety, you will not easily bolt it again, but it can be done. Two ferrets entered in the bury will press the rabbit hard and it may make a mistake. Moreover if it takes refuge in another bury, it is on foreign territory, and rabbits are very territorial. They will not tolerate a strange rabbit in their bury, and when you put your ferret in the new bury, there is every chance that 'your' rabbit will be the first out, probably to dash back to its real home, where it will backnet itself.

You might also enter two ferrets together when the bury size is such that you feel one ferret is having to work too hard going after rabbits that do not feel the need to bolt. Two ferrets certainly increase the pressure on the rabbits. There is a slightly higher risk of a kill under if they trap the rabbit between them, but with a larger bury, or to evict a last, elusive rabbit, two ferrets have more than twice the effectiveness of one.

A bury on a hillside probably does not have a great deal of cover, and rabbits will tend to pop out of one hole straight back down another. This is a situation when you should either go armed with plenty of purse nets, or else with a gun on your own. Send your ferret in, take up your stance on the opposite side, and pick the rabbits off as they present themselves. The small patches of cover on the hillside tend to contain smallish buries, and the rabbits will run from one patch of cover to the next.

A big bury which would need a lot of purse nets – or one long net.

You may have a long walk from where you leave your car to where you start to ferret, so be sure to secure and immobilise your vehicle. Take care near public footpaths: there are people who love the countryside as a concept but have little idea of what makes it tick, and cannot cope with the reality of fluffy bunnies being culled. This can mean a vandalised car, which is not the perfect end to the day.

This bury is in the middle of the thistles – and a long way from the car for carrying equipment.

Rules need to be flexible, and one of the most flexible concerns silence and the clearing of heavy cover prior to ferreting. Although I have stressed the need for silence when working a bury, it is impossible to clear cover quietly. However, it is inadvisable to clear cover and then ferret a day or two later, as one of two things could happen. The rabbits may move out because they feel insecure, or someone else may ferret your newly cleared bury for you. There is likely to be someone like this in almost every area that you cover, and they possess an unnerving instinct for knowing when someone has cleared a bury. So clear it and ferret it in the same day, and then you reap the reward for all your hard work.

*Ferrets can get
very wet and
muddy
underground.*

*This one
followed rabbits
into water.*

If the bury borders a stream, watch for escape holes in the side
of the bank. Rabbits do not like getting wet, but they are bigger
than ferrets, and will sometimes take refuge below the water
line where the ferret cannot follow. If your ferret comes out
soaking wet, then it is likely that the rabbit is sitting in deeper
water than your ferret wants to tackle. Do not force the issue,
for although ferrets can and do swim, the rabbit will struggle
and kick, and you do not want to risk your ferret drowning.

Sometimes your ferret will kill under and drag the rabbit out, and sometimes she will drag out a live rabbit. Precisely how a one-pound ferret intends to deal with a three-pound rabbit once she has it outside, I am not sure but the strength involved in simply bringing the rabbit out is incredible when one considers that the rabbit is clinging to the sides of the tunnel as hard as it can. Watch for any unusual movement of your nets, or of a ferret emerging slowly and jerkily backwards, and assist her by getting hold of the rabbit as soon as you can, but be careful that you do not get a nip from the ferret! Kill the rabbit quickly, and then let your ferret rag the carcase for a minute or two as her reward. She will not damage the meat you want, as she will stick to the head, and once she is quite satisfied that the rabbit is dead, she will lose interest in it and go down to find another one.

Ferrets are very strong. This one has no intention of letting go of the rabbit, although it is dead.

The chances are that your landowner will want you to kill every rabbit that you can, although a lot of ferreters let small rabbits go. Rabbits in the early stages are incredibly appealing, but remember that they will be breeding in a very few weeks, and their mother is already pregnant again. As the guest of your landowner, you must follow his wishes; modern farming means that land is always in production, and so are rabbits. A word of warning: you will come across people who will ask you to supply live rabbits. Do not agree. Whatever they want them for it is likely to be illegal and inhumane. If this is a condition of your permission, I recommend that you go ferreting elsewhere.

This small ferret dragged this big rabbit out of the bury.

There is nothing like local knowledge, and as you build up your experience on the land you hunt regularly you will become more successful. You can only get out of a bury what is in there in the first place, and if it is only one rabbit do not feel demoralised. On the other hand, if you get one rabbit out, it is likely that there will be another one, unless the rabbit is old or sick, in which case it may well have been rejected by the main colony.

Let your ferret worry a dead rabbit as a reward.

How soon you can ferret a bury again depends on the local rabbit population. If this is excessive, then new rabbits will take it over within a couple of weeks: at other times, it may remain empty for some months. If big buries are being ferreted, refugee rabbits may take cover in smaller buries nearby. The rabbit population will fluctuate with the season, the weather, myxomatosis or other diseases, and the degree to which they are being harried by dogs, guns or ferrets. I know of one farmer who acquired a brace of lurcher pups; within six months they were hunting, and for the next two years rabbits were being so harassed that they only lived on the farm boundaries. After the young bitch was rehomed, because she was starting to wander in search of more rabbits, the dog would only hunt if someone took him, and the rabbits started to come back. So keep abreast of what is happening with the rabbits on your permission land, and soon you will develop the knack of being in the right place at the right time, which is as much a skill as any other aspect of being a ferreter.

Myxomatosis. No ferreting to be had here.

Chapter Seven

The Group Experience

The essence of the ferreter is silence: he comes, he goes, and the landscape bears little sign of his passing, except that there are fewer rabbits. Although very large buries can be tackled by several ferreters, for the most part ferreting is undertaken by one or two people, aided perhaps by a dog or a gun. I have seen a ruthless team of six in action: two clearing the buries with a swap-hook and secateurs, two setting nets and two ferreting, and a lot of land was covered that day. Mostly, however, ferreting, like fishing, is a solitary occupation, and tends not to attract the sort of person who is happiest in a group. Yet ferret clubs exist and thrive, and I recommend that you join your local ferret group, for a number of reasons.

An organised group of ferreters has much more chance of gaining rabbiting permission than an individual. Once the word begins to spread that the ferret club does a good job and is respectful of the land, more and more permission will come the way of that group. Any club so placed, with a growing reputation to safeguard, will instil a code of good conduct in its new members, and the image of ferreting as a whole can only benefit. When you start to seek hunting permission, and it seems an uphill task, you will hear over and over that ferreters are no longer welcome on the land because of others' bad behaviour. This can range from carelessness in filling in diggings or clearing buries – if you clear an area of bramble and whin so that you can ferret, the landowner will not be best pleased to find it dumped in a ditch or piled up in his arable fields – to heinous crimes such as killing pheasants or damaging crops. A ferret club has much more chance of securing permission under these circumstances than an individual, because the landowner will feel that an organised group with a good reputation is less of a risk than a complete stranger. There are even instances where professional pest controllers make use of their local ferret club to contract out work at busy times.

The club to which I belong does promotional work at country shows in the summer, and has a constant stream of enquiries from people who need help with a rabbit problem. These shows, as well as being tremendous fun, are a good vehicle for presenting the ferret and the ferreter to the public. We have one main ring demonstration that involves a bury constructed from artificial grass and plastic pipes, a toy rabbit and a real ferret, which always brings the house down! The ferrets meet a lot of people, and prove that they are not the stinking, vicious creatures that people may think they are and the ferreters prove that they are not furtive poachers. Any landowner meeting clean, friendly ferrets and polite, friendly ferreters is more than halfway to allowing members of the club on his land.

A club of any sort is only as good as its committee and its members. If the word 'committee' makes you shudder, bear in mind that, for your own credibility and protection, you need a degree of formality in your club, even if it just sets out to be a group of friends who are looking for some ferreting. You must have insurance: it is vital that the group is covered against litigation for injury, accidental damage or any other problems. It is a rare gentlemen's agreement that stays gentlemanly when something unforeseen arises. With insurance, landowners will welcome you and be impressed with your professional outlook; without it, you will have problems. If your club is affiliated to the British Field Sports Society (BFSS) – and it should be – under the current arrangements you are insured for injury and third-party liability incurred while ferreting, with other options available on request. If, however, you participate as I do in ferret displays and demonstrations to which the public has access, you must extend your insurance cover accordingly. This is where the committee comes in.

The insurance company will want to see that your club is properly run and regulated. A formal constitution (it need only be a simple one, but there must be one), a treasurer who can present the club's financial status in a universally understood manner and other committee members as needed go a long way to proving that. It is essential to have an AGM at which paid-up members have a voice and a vote, and decisions pertaining to the club's affairs may be democratically discussed. If all this seems excessive for a group of friends with a common interest in ferrets, believe me it is necessary. Although your treasurer and members may be absolutely honest, anything can happen, and in some clubs it already has! The constitution and formal committee structure protects the club and its members, and ensures the continuation of the democratic process. Members should have the liberty to become involved as little or as much as they wish, according to their commitments and priorities. A newsletter is not essential, but it is always well received and is a good way of keeping everyone up to date with the activities of the club as well as news that is of interest from the outside world. For instance, when Aleutian disease (explained in detail in Chapter II) first became known in this country as a ferret disease, it was the ferret clubs that liaised with the veterinary profession and each other, and by pooling information and initiating voluntary restrictions on the movements of ferrets, helped to prevent it from becoming an epidemic.

I mentioned affiliation to the BFSS. Every ferret club should be a member, for this is the organisation that protects our liberty to go ferreting. Ferreting is a humane and efficient method of pest control, yet there are groups that are trying to get it banned, and that do not hesitate to harass and sometimes attack people who are out ferreting. If we want to retain the marvellous freedom we have in these islands to go ferreting whenever we wish and wherever we have permission, then joining the BFSS is a small price to pay bearing in mind what we have to lose. Those of us who shoot would be wise to join the British Association for Shooting and Conservation (BASC) as well, and many country sports supporters are members of both.

What other advantages are there in joining a club? You will find a ready supply of well-bred ferrets when you need to add to your stock, there will be vasectomised hobs available for members' jills, a thriving second-hand market in ferreting equipment, books and videos, and people who make nets and hutches and who can show you how to do it if you want to learn or sell you some if you want to buy. There may be discounts on bulk purchases of ferret food – day-old chicks, for example, which have to be bought in quantity, or surplus rabbits donated in times of plenty, for the use of those who would like to feed their ferrets on rabbit but do not want to go ferreting. Many clubs have a ferret-friendly and ferret-owning vet who can supply health information, and perhaps group vaccination for members' ferrets. Some clubs have a very active social side while others are quieter, but all of them can offer something to the working ferreter. After all that we get out of our ferreting, it is nice to be able to put something back in, and some clubs are very active on the ferret welfare side, both with rescuing and rehoming lost or abandoned ferrets, and with PR work. It is surprising what an attraction a few friendly ferrets can be at a show or similar event and the ferrets seem to enjoy all the activity as well. Helpful advice on ferret care and maintenance is always available to new or prospective ferret owners, and the club often ends the day with one or two new members. Showing and ferret racing are not to everyone's taste, but a lot of people thoroughly enjoy both, and it keeps the ferrets fit and amused through the summer, for a lot of people only ferret in the winter months. My vasectomised hob ferret was banned from the ferret racing one summer, as his romantic liaisons had kept him so lean and fit that he just kept on winning!

Chapter Eight

Shooting over Ferrets

Shooting over ferrets will enable you to cover more ground in less time than other methods, because you are saved the chores of clearing undergrowth round the buries and setting and taking up nets. There is less disturbance to the bury, as you only go near it to introduce the ferret, and so there is no need for the settling down period required after laying purse nets. There is no need to run across the bury to pick up a netted rabbit and reset the net, and usually no need to kill the rabbit by hand. I ferreted for a shooting man one day and discovered that he simply could not kill by hand; he had never had to, and did not know how.

What sort of gun is best for shooting over ferrets? Anything between a .410 and a 12-bore that you are familiar and comfortable with. People will tell you that you should use nothing smaller than No.5 shot, but in fact it is perfectly possible to use light-load 7s in your 20-bore, or 2/5 ounce of shot in a 2½ inch .410, so if that is your preference, that is what you should use. Rabbits will bolt in rapid succession, so if your chosen type of shotgun is a pump or automatic, it may be worth having a firearms certificate rather than just a shotgun licence, as the latter limits you to a maximum of three cartridges in use at a time – two in the magazine and one in the chamber. You will therefore have more flexibility and avoid the frustration of losing rabbits because you cannot load fast enough.

An assortment of guns suitable for shooting over ferrets. Left to right: 12-bore side-by-side, 20-bore over-and-under, single-barrel .410, pump-action, .410, 12-bore automatic.

As with any other shooting activity, safety must be on your mind the whole time. The ideal arrangement is for one person to handle the ferrets and one to shoot, but it is perfectly possible to do both yourself, or for several Guns to be out. Always be aware of what is around you in the way of footpaths (people do not always stick to them), livestock and buildings, and remember the risk of ricochet, especially when the ground is hard. Dogs should be left at home unless they are very steady, in which case a reliable gundog type will be useful for retrieving after shooting at a particular bury has finished. Refrain from shooting a cautious rabbit that sits at the entrance to the bury, deciding what to do for the best, as the ferret might be right behind it. Unless you are absolutely sure of where the ferrets are, only shoot bolting rabbits.

Try to position yourself so that you shoot rabbits as they cross in front of you rather than bolting away from you. The target area is then larger and more vulnerable. You should try to avoid maiming rabbits, and one that is shot from behind will often drag itself a long way, possibly down a hole. There is an old saying that 'if you shoot the head, the arse dies, but if you shoot the arse, the head don't die', so shoot the head or the middle, and then all of it dies. Remember, too, that a dead rabbit's nervous reflex can cause quite a bit of kicking and jumping, especially with a head shot, and a rabbit can kick itself down a hole and be lost to you.

If a ferret lies up and must be dug down to, see that the person shooting is alert and ready, for rabbits will often bolt while the dig is in progress. But so will a lot of other creatures, so check before you start what your permission covers. Keepered land will probably need all predators kept down, and you will therefore be honour bound to despatch stoats, foxes, rats and mink. At buries in good hunting country you may have to leave foxes alone, while arable farmers might want everything except rats left, as the foxes and mustelids will be keeping the rabbits down, and the livestock and poultry farmer will probably want all legal quarry despatched.

The rabbits that you shoot will be less saleable than those caught in nets or by a soft-mouthed dog. Gunshot rabbits are perfectly acceptable dog and ferret food. Do not worry about the effects of lead shot on your animals; ferrets are small enough to spit the shot out, which you will discover when you clean their hutch, and as dogs are better fed on cooked rabbit taken off the bone, you will be able to remove the shot yourself. It has to be said that paunching shot rabbits is not for the squeamish, and you will get your hands dirty, but after that is done, you have pounds of beautiful meat ready for use, and you can always wash your hands.

Good buries for shooting over. The rabbits will run to the patches of cover.

Shooting over ferrets is best done across open land where visibility is good, or in areas of thick cover which it would be impractical to clear. Rabbits that bolt always know where they are going, and it is to the next area of cover. They may rattle around in the brambles for quite some time before they break, and they will not be slow once they do, but they will not jink and spin the way the would with a dog behind them, because they do not know that you are there with the gun. Hedgerows are difficult because the rabbits tend to bolt along the hedge rather than leaving its shelter, and Guns shooting hedgerows must be very disciplined to avoid accidents.

The rabbits that leave the bury as soon as the ferret goes in are not particularly frightened, merely taking the precaution of quitting an area that now has something unpleasant in it, but those that take on a ferret underground, or that bolt and are coursed by a dog, or are shot and wounded will have had a sufficient fright to use their musk glands, and will smell strongly. Rabbits that have been caught in live traps smell terrible from their fear, and the stench taints the meat. Your dogs and ferrets will not mind but humans will, so this should be borne in mind when you select rabbits for human consumption.

Getting ready to start.

Let us look at a typical day shooting over ferrets. The ferrets are experienced, and not frightened by gunfire because their handler has started them tactfully, and has never taken them hunting with anyone who was likely to shoot a rabbit close to a ferret. Your gun is an old friend, with which you are both confident and comfortable, and you have the ammunition that you prefer. You are carrying the correct paperwork for your gun, your written permission to hunt on the land, plenty of ammunition and a good knife. Your friend has brought ferrets, locators and the graft. The landowner has asked that you shoot any vermin that you see, and that you contact him when you have finished. Although there are hedgerow buries here, you will be working the hillside ones in the field, which afford you a clear view. Rabbits will bolt from these buries to the hedge on one side and the woods at right angles, so you have a good idea of where to stand. No stock is out, and although it is cold, the ground is not frozen. As you take up position, your friend, who has already collared up the ferrets and tested the locator, gently places a polecat jill at the bottom entrance of the nearest bury, which looks well used. She does not hesitate, but goes straight in, and you can hear your own heart beating.

Things start happening almost at once. Quite far along the bury, a wise old rabbit is sitting in the entrance to its home, its nose twitching as it tests the air. You have approached down-wind and are discreetly dressed; you stand motionless and the rabbit does not know you are there. Cautiously it hops once, twice, pauses and washes one ear. Still you do not move. Then, close to you, a rabbit bolts like a cork out of a bottle, straight across, and somersaults to the gun that you are barely aware of having raised and fired. While you are doing so, the old buck has popped underground again. Now it knows the nature of the game, and no ferret will shift it. It has shouldered into a stop end, its wide rump filling the tunnel completely, and the only way that you will get this fellow out is to dig. Meanwhile, rabbits are bolting well. Two come out of the same hole and break to left and right. You shoot one and the other makes it to the safety of the woods. You are very busy for a while, and then the jill comes out, rears up to see where her owner is and then proceeds with her ungainly looping gait to the next group of rabbit holes.

Your friend is picking up the rabbits, draining and hocking them, and hanging them in pairs, belly fur out to cool the viscera and be more easily seen. Dead rabbits are best picked up as soon as possible; if you do not, you will only supply an unexpected bounty to a stoat, badger or fox. Normally, you would help your friend with the rabbits, but something is bothering the jill, which has backed out spitting and cackling, with her tail a-fizz. You know better than to force her back in, or indeed handle her at all, for she is very agitated. Presently, she goes into another hole, but you barely notice as something odd is filling the hole she has just come from. Grey-brown and untidy, moodily clicking to itself, it shows itself as a little owl disturbed from its nap. It runs across the grass surprisingly quickly with its flat-footed sailor's roll, before taking to the air.

Relaxing between buries.

After she has been through the next bury, the jill's owner takes her up, offers her a drink of weak milk and water, and boxes her up for a rest. Now it is the turn of the white jill. She is big and mean, flies to ground and locks onto the old buck, which was beginning to relax. There is a lot of thumping as she tries to get it out. It is wedged solidly in, so that she cannot climb over its back and kill it with a head bite, as a smaller ferret might with a smaller rabbit, so she scratches furiously at its quarters, bites its rump and tries to pull it out. She knows that if she stays with it, the graft will soon dig down to her, and she is right, for her owner has read the situation. As he digs, you are ready with the gun, and sure enough, you are able to get another bolter. Where had it been, that the good polecat jill had missed it? Probably high on a shelf, or tucked into another stop end. The polecat does not stay with a rabbit but the white does, and it is useful to send another ferret through the bury to tidy up after the first one has done her bit. They all work differently, and a good handler uses this to his advantage.

You work steadily along the slope until you reach the wood, and then you hear a rabbit squealing. As quietly as possible, your friend picks his way through the trees, and then turns, grinning, beckoning you to come quickly. In the clearing at the top, a stoat is clinging to a bucking, squealing rabbit. Both are oblivious to your approach; the rabbit, fighting for its life and yelling as hard as it can, is leaping and kicking, snapping the tiny stoat backwards and forwards like a whip, but the stoat will not loosen her grip at the back of the rabbit's head. Presently, the rabbit freezes, its squealing dies to a rattling gasp, its eyes glaze, and it keels over. The stoat shakes it like a diminutive terrier, but as the bloodlust cools in her, she smells that humans are close by, and makes to run off. The landowner's instructions were clear, and the stoat is shot as he requested. She is a pretty creature, with her bright chestnut and white fur, and the characteristic black tip to her tail – this far south, stoats do not change in winter to the ermine white of their northern relatives – but she and her kin are over-abundant here, and causing problems to ground-nesting birds.

So, you have a rabbit that did not cost you a cartridge, and one that is fit for sale or human consumption, as the only damage is the stoat's killing bite at the back of its neck. As you go back into the wood, a strong smell of fox and a steaming dropping indicate that you were not the only predators to be attracted by the squealing rabbit.

The end of a successful morning shooting over ferrets.

Finally, it is time to pack up and go home. As you retrace your steps, you pick up any cartridge cases that you may have overlooked earlier, and collect the pairs of rabbits from the trees and fences on which they have been hung. You dig a hole, paunch out the catch and bury the paunch. The fox may find it later. As you finish, and are wiping your hands on the grass, a rat runs across in front of you, and your friend, a fine snap-shooter, kills it with one shot. It is a big buck rat, balding and bloated, looking close to the end of its natural span.

85

You call in at the house to say that you have finished, and offer a brace of good rabbits to the landowner. He takes note of the fox's visit, and is as pleased about the demise of the stoat and the rat as he is about the rabbit tally. It is a good job done, and you are most welcome to return whenever you want.

Chapter Nine

Ferrets and Lurchers

Working a lurcher and ferrets together is a delight. Traditionally a 'whirrier' – half-whippet half-terrier – is used, the most sought-after being the Bedlington/whippet cross. However, I have seen raking greyhound/deerhound crosses working well, and one of the best ferreting dogs I have ever seen is a pure-bred saluki from generations of show stock. Almost any dog will do the job as long as she is silent, obedient, and has lightning kick-off speed. A rabbit's sprint from bury to covert is rarely more than 50 yards, so a dog that takes time to get into top gear will lose you rabbits unless she has other lethal skills at her disposal – as some do, of which more later. She also needs to be mature enough to maintain her concentration for long periods of time, which is why I have always taught ferreting after the dog has mastered other hunting methods. Only once have I tried doing it the other way around, and it gave me some interesting training problems as the dog expected me to produce a ferret every time a rabbit had gone to ground, but it was all resolved in due course. No one knows your dog the way you do, and they are all different, so by all means teach ferreting first if she is mentally strong enough to take it.

A purebred saluki retrieves a rabbit live to hand.

The dog must be seen to be steady to ferrets. Some people like to introduce pups to ferret kits over a bowl of milk, and it must work for them because they keep on doing it, but I find several drawbacks to this approach. You need to have pups and kits at the same time, which is difficult in itself and impossible if you have an adult dog which you will be starting from scratch. Moreover both pups and kits can be possessive about the milk, which may lead to the very situation that you are trying to avoid. Milk is also a savage laxative, so that your ferret hutch and puppy pen are going to need attention afterwards.

For me, the following is the best way to introduce dogs and ferrets. Put the dog on a lead and hold the ferret in your hand. Allow them to sniff each other, but don't let the ferret nip the dog, and tell the dog to leave it if she attempts to lunge at or mouth the ferret. When they are used to each other in this situation, let the ferret run about on a harness and line, with the dog still on a lead or tied up. When the dog is calm about this, loose her and make her lie down while the ferret plays near her, still on its line because you do not want your dog nipped. Finally, loose them both in a confined area, closely supervised, until you are satisfied that the dog is reliable. Some ferrets are never reliable with dogs, as they regard every animal as food. (I know one that once took on a pony, and my white jill went running after a sheep last year), but lurchers are very easy to break to ferret. Other breeds are different so be careful, especially with terriers. Above all, never trust an unknown dog, no matter what its owner says – many ferrets have been killed this way.

Once the dog is steady to the ferret, she must learn to mark rabbit buries, i.e. test the entrances for scent, and indicate to you whether or not there are rabbits inside. She must be unobtrusive so that the rabbits are not terrified into staying underground, so you do not want the scrabbling and yapping of a pet dog. A working dog delicately flowers her nostrils rather in the manner of a connoisseur of fine wine, assesses the contents of the bury, and transmits the information to you by body language. Different dogs do this in different ways: my old bitch will stare intently at the bury and then back at me if the rabbits are deep inside, but if they are near the surface and ready to bolt, she will wag her tail and back away, dancing up on her toes and pleading with her eyes for me to put a ferret in. If the bury is empty, she will not even glance at me, but will carry on trying holes until she meets with success. Trust your dog and you will save a lot of time, because you will not be netting up empty buries. And no matter how disused a bury looks, if your dog says that there are rabbits inside, believe her.

How do you teach this? The answer is you do not. Your dog will teach you. Watch her when you are walking along rabbit buries, and see her different reactions to the holes she sniffs at.

You will soon understand when a hole is occupied, and that is the time to bring along a ferret. Do not use nets at this stage, for you want the dog to realise that when you put a ferret in, it means a rabbit will come out, and then she will have some fun. Once the ferret is down, gently hold the dog in a standing position by the bury, and release her as soon as a rabbit bolts. If the rabbit's exit is fast, let her go at once; if the rabbit is the cautious sort that comes out by degrees, do not slip her until it is clear of the bury and can give her a run. She will not take long to learn, and it does not matter if she does not catch the rabbit, as long as she enjoys herself.

The only reward for the mark must be the bolting of the rabbit. If you praise her for marking, she will start to 'false mark' – i.e. mark every bury, whether occupied or not, because she wants to please you and it is her perception that it is the act of marking that does so. Once she understands what happens when the ferret goes in, you will be able to rely upon her utterly. My old bitch taught her own pup to mark, and if they are out together, despite the fact that the 'pup' is now a middle-aged dog, the mother will bustle up and confirm every mark that the younger dog makes, rather like one pointer backing another.

After your dog has learned what ferrets do, introduce her to the nets. I am talking about purse nets, as training a long-netting dog is a rare accomplishment these days, and would warrant a chapter to itself. Net some of the rabbit holes, but not all of them, and tell her 'no' if she attempts to paw the nets. Some people like a dog to stand off a netted coney, others to pin it in the net until they can get to it. I am one of the latter sort, as you cannot rely on the rabbits to bolt singly, and it is useful when working on your own if the dog will hold one while you attend to another. Some dogs pin with their paws, others with their mouths, and it does not matter which she does as long as she does not crunch the rabbit. So if a rabbit bolts, let her course it; if it is netted, let her pounce on it if you want it pinned, or tell her to leave it if you want it left.

One of the author's lurchers listening to the action underground.

Once the rabbit is dead, she must not touch it, for which I use the command 'no-dead'. You will be surprised at how easily she will learn, but bear in mind that, to start with, you are going to lose some rabbits. When she has retrieved one that she has coursed and caught, do not snatch it from her. Some

91

lurchers are shy retrievers, and it is very easy to sicken them of it completely. So take the rabbit tactfully, praise and make a fuss of her, and if doing this causes you to lose a rabbit, console yourself with the thought that there will be others. Better that than losing a whole lot more in the future while you chase your lurcher around the field trying to get one off her just because you bungled her first catch and retrieve.

When she will mark buries, do what you want with netted conies, catch and retrieve bolters, now comes the professionalism. This is when she goes from apprentice to journeyman, and thence to master craftsman.

She will stand poised over the bury, ears flicking, following the movements underground with her superior hearing, feeling the vibrations under her feet as the ferret and rabbits travel the underground corridors. Some lurchers will mark where the ferret is holding a rabbit so that you can dig down to them. Some will even dig for you! Some will snatch a fleeing coney from the mouth of the burrow, so that you do not even need to net, so accurately do they predict where the rabbit will bolt from. I watched Brian Plummer's *Merab* do this one day in Scotland; twenty-six rabbits bolted, twenty-six rabbits were caught by this grey-muzzled old bitch, then in her tenth year. She did not course one of them and we did not set one net – every rabbit was swept up as it left the rabbit hole.

If you train your dog carefully for ferreting, you will have a companion more useful than another human, but remember their attention span. If you have a big bury to net, and a young dog with you, do not be ashamed to tie her up while you net, and release her from the discipline of lie-and-stay for an hour. If you net every rabbit hole and never allow her a catch, she will become bored, and boredom in a young dog equals either mischief or non-co-operation. Let her play her part and have her fun, and she will serve you well into old age. And remember that rabbits bolted by a ferret are not as fast as lamped rabbits, and a dog that has become too slow for lamped rabbits will still have enough rabbit sense as well as enough speed to be a useful ferreting dog.

Not very long ago, I was ferreting a bury on baked hard clay soil, where getting the pegs of the nets into the ground was almost beyond me. The nets served only to delay the rabbits, but my young lurcher scooped up every coney as it bolted, and held it for me. I could not have dug if I had wanted to, as the ground was so hard, but my two show-bred jills worked the bury like the experts they are and came out to me when they had finished, and my headstrong, sensitive bitch, who has been the very devil to train, worked flawlessly. Working lurchers and ferrets together, as long as you have done your ground-work carefully, is indeed a delight.

Chapter Ten

The Catch

Ferreting involves catching rabbits, and you need to know what to do with them. Once they are caught you owe it to them to kill them quickly and humanely, and there are several ways to do this.

The 'rabbit punch' is a bit of a cliché. It is probably the least efficient of the methods we use, as it requires a degree of strength, but if you want to try it, hold the rabbit up by its hind legs and strike it as hard as you can with the side of your hand to the vulnerable area where the neck joins the back of the head. A better way, however is chinning, where you hold the rabbit round the neck with one hand, pressing with your knuckles into the back of the head, and push smartly up under the chin with your other hand. Correctly done, this causes a 'hangman's fracture' of the highest vertebra where it supports the head.

*Coup de grâce 1:
holding the rabbit
round the neck and
the hindlegs.*

*Coup de grâce 2:
holding the rabbit
in front of the
ears, which is
easier for smaller
people.*

96

The easiest method for people who are not very strong is to hold the rabbit round the hind legs with one hand, close the other hand firmly round his head in front of the ears, being careful that the rabbit does not bite you, and pull the head up with a sharp jerk. You will feel either the neck break or the spinal cord go. You can also hold the rabbit's hind legs in one hand and grip it behind the ears, which is sometimes more convenient, but requires a little extra strength. If the rabbit is large and you have short arms, you can gain extra leverage by stretching it across your knee.

I have also seen rabbits killed instantly by holding them by the head and snapping their bodies like a whip, which again breaks the neck, and I know people who like to use a priest – a weighted piece of wood, deer antler or something similar, which is used to strike the back of the head. Whichever method you use, there can be a surprising amount of kicking and twitching in a recently killed animal, so ensure that you have done the job properly by dabbing a finger at the rabbit's eye and checking the blink reflex.

Now you must drain out the urine. Once the carcase has fully slackened, and preferably before rigor mortis sets in, hold it with the tail down and underside away from you, place your thumbs firmly over the centre of its abdomen and press inwards and downwards at the same time, drawing your thumbs down until they reach the genitals. Unless the rabbit was very frightened before it died, you will push a stream of urine out of it, which would otherwise taint the meat.

It is traditional to 'hock' rabbits and hang them up to cool while you are ferreting, and the sooner they cool, the better the meat. Rabbit is a meat which definitely does not improve with keeping, and is best used as fresh as possible. Feel the hind leg just above the hock, and find the gap between the hock and the tendon. With your knife, make a slit in this gap that is big enough to push the other hind foot through. Take care to confine your cut to the membrane; do not damage the meat by sliding your knife too high. Once hocked, the rabbit can be hung up until you are ready to paunch out your catch.

The paunch should come out as soon as possible, but it is not a good idea to handle ferrets with hands that smell of rabbit guts, so do this once you have finished for the day, and the ferrets have been given their drink and are boxed up ready for the trip home.

The idea is to get the viscera out without puncturing them. Hold the rabbit head up and underside out, and either make a small slit in the belly fur which you then split longwise with your fingers, or hold up a section of fur between finger and thumb and cut off the piece of skin that you are holding. Either of these methods will open the hide and leave intact the membrane which holds the guts. With a sharp knife and enough practice you can slice through skin and membrane in one go, but it is easy to pierce the guts as well, so be careful until you master the technique. Carefully run the tip of your knife from top to bottom of the membrane, and the guts will tumble out after the knife. At the bottom of the ribcage, the liver and the stomach lie together; gently, with fingers or knife, ease the stomach sac clear of the liver and remove it, leaving the liver intact inside the rabbit. Stomach sacs have a way of bursting and showering you with their evil-smelling contents, so be warned! At the other end of the carcase, a small length of intestine will be clinging to the rabbit's rectum, so knock that clear with your knife. Some people are adroit at flicking the viscera out of the rabbit, and if your hunting companion is one of these, be careful where you stand. The advantage of this method is that your hands stay cleaner. Rabbit guts have a smell that will cling through baths and all manner of disinfectants. A container of baby wipes in the car will save making the steering wheel sticky, but I afraid you will be stuck with the stink until much later. The disadvantages are that you spread the guts over quite a wide area, you can lose the liver along with the stomach, and you do not get much of a chance to examine the viscera.

But why do you need to look at the viscera? You need to know how healthy the rabbit is before you allocate it for human, dog or ferret consumption. Are there white spots on the liver? Are liver or kidneys misshapen, discoloured or pulpy? If so, the meat should not be eaten by humans. Is the rabbit pregnant? Rabbit foetuses were known in the old days as 'laurices', and permitted fare on Fridays when meat was not to be consumed for religious reasons. But I do not recommend that you offer them for human consumption. Give them to your ferrets, who will appreciate them much more. Is there a tapeworm? Rabbits play host to some impressive specimens. Take care not to touch the worm, and earmark the rabbit as not for human consumption. If you decide to feed it to the dogs after you have removed the worm, make sure that the flesh is thoroughly cooked. Always take cooked rabbit meat off the bone for dogs, as the bones are hard and splintery, and could prove fatal.

When you have paunched the rabbits and disposed of the paunch carefully as required, it is time to take your catch home and prepare it for the table.

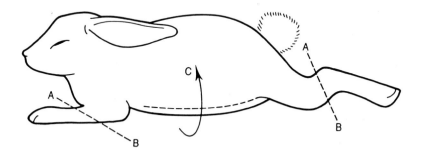

Figure 4. Skinning a rabbit
(a) Cut through the legs across AB. Loosen the belly skin from the paunching, cut upwards towards the backbone.

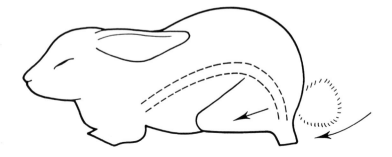

(b) Push each hind leg forward out of the skin.

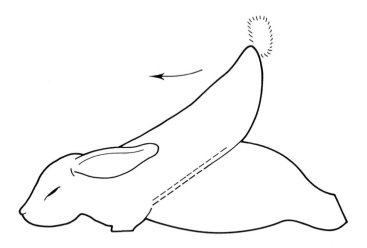

(c) Cut through the tailbone at A, and pull the skin towards rabbit's head.

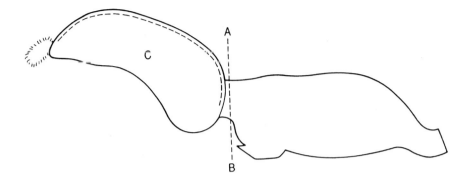

(d) Push the skin C right over the head and cut through the neck at AB.

(e) Location of musk glands A. Slit the membrane and remove these.

Separating a rabbit from its skin is the easiest of tasks. I prefer to skin a warm rabbit, others would rather tackle the task after rigor mortis has worn off, but you will get plenty of practice either way. I cut off the hind legs at the hock and the front ones at the wrist before I start. Secateurs or a cleaver make this job easy. Then take the skin where you have opened the rabbit's belly, and pull it away from the flesh until you have loosened the skin on both sides right up to the backbone. Do not pull too hard, or you might break the spine. Push one back leg up while you push the skin away, and it will easily slip out. Then do the same with the other hind leg, and cut around the bone of the tail to free the whole hindquarter. Now you can pull the skin forward like a jumper over the rabbit's head. Cut through the neck, and give the head to the ferrets. In the old days, people would skin the head and eat that too, but we are not so hungry any more! An alternative way to skin a rabbit is to cut the skin across the back and pull it off in two or four sections, the bottom half down and the top half up.

Ferreted rabbits ready for skinning.

When you are getting a lot of rabbits, you will probably prefer to feed the fore end to the ferrets and keep the meatier part from the bottom of the ribcage backwards for your dog and yourself. Either side of the rabbit's spine is a succulent fillet, and the hind legs also carry a lot of flesh. As an · animal that has to run for its life every day, the rabbit does not carry belly flesh. If it has fed well, especially on a cereal crop, it may carry bright yellow fat under the skin and around the internal organs; this is perfectly safe to eat if you wish.

If you are preparing rabbit for the table, you should remove the two musk glands which are situated right at the top of the hind legs. These greyish-green oval glands are about the size of peas, and will taint the meat if you cook the rabbit with them *in situ*. With the skinned rabbit on its back, pull the tailbone up, which will make the glands protrude slightly. Free them from their position just under the skin, and scoop them out with the point of your knife. Then, with the rabbit still on its back, split the pubic bone between the hind legs before removing the genitalia and the remnants of the intestinal debris. If the whole of the rabbit is destined for human consumption, open the membrane which covers the chest cavity at the bottom of the ribcage, and remove the heart and lungs.

To joint the rabbit, cut across the spine at the pelvis and again at the bottom of the ribcage, which separates the saddle, and then cut along the spine to give two shoulder and two hind-leg joints. Alternatively, joint the back legs as before and leave the saddle attached to the forepart of the rabbit; this is the better way with small rabbits.

As with most meats, young rabbit is much nicer than old, and it is worth the extra trouble of skinning two tender young ones rather than a tough old buck. Young rabbits have soft, easily torn ears and pliable feet, and you will find them much easier to skin. A blunt-headed, battle-scarred old buck will really stick to the pelt, and you may safely assume that if it is a struggle to skin, it will not be the sweetest of eating. However, if a tough old rabbit is all you have, soak it in salt water for several hours, and be sure to remove the jelly-like membrane from the flesh before you cook it. If you have a milky doe, she will be perfectly good to eat, although unsaleable as people are prejudiced against the idea of eating a suckling animal.

People will tell you that rabbit tastes just like chicken. It does not; it tastes just like rabbit. Mrs Beeton lists it under 'poultry' probably because the meat is white, but the robustly musky savour of rabbit is not to everyone's liking. Some people like to soak rabbit in milk for a few hours before rinsing it off and cooking it, and it is certainly improved for soaking in salt water. Only use one of these methods, however, as the two together would definitely not work. Very young rabbits – the sort that almost slip through the nets – can be delicious sautéd in butter or olive oil, but maturer rabbit is best when casseroled exquisitely slowly with onion, mushrooms and winter vegetables.

I have eaten rabbit cooked with tripe in Portugal, and it was a much pleasanter experience than it sounds, while the French find rabbit an ideal vehicle for the rich, velvety cream or butter sauces in which they specialise. If you fear for the state of your arteries, you can eschew lush sauces quite cheerfully, for wild rabbit is low in fat and easily digested, and will casserole sensationally in cider or white wine. The best herbs are basil and bay, and a dash of nutmeg will balance and enhance the flavour beautifully. Pork sausage-meat balls, chestnut stuffing, bacon or ham (real ham of course, taken off the bone) all make a tasty addition to a dish of rabbit. If you are very slowly casseroling an old one, perhaps for a pie, a couple of pieces of oxtail and a dash of Worcester sauce will have everyone hanging around for second helpings. One of my farmer friends makes the following delicious autumn jelly to serve with game, which you might like to try.

Jo Lundgren's Autumn Jelly

Ingredients
2lb blackberries
1lb sloes
1lb elderberries
2lb crab apples
1 lemon
Pectin
1 – 2lb preserving sugar

Method

Slowly simmer all the fruit except the lemon in 2 pints of water until it is pulped. Strain through muslin (do not sieve) and for a tangy mixture add sugar to the pulp in the proportion 2 pints pulp to 1 pint sugar – actually measured out in the pint jug. If you have a sweet tooth, add more sugar, but not more than the amount of pulp. Add the juice of one lemon and the pectin, and boil for eight minutes. Test for setting, and put into jars.

This autumn jelly is a glowing, dark ruby colour, and absolutely delicious with hot or cold game. Half the fun is in the gathering of the ingredients, which has been made much easier by the invention of the freezer, as it is a rare year when they all come ready together.

Not all of us have the time or inclination for this sort of cooking, and a few slices of lemon or a Bramley cooking apple will improve your rabbit with little effort on your part. I always feel that rabbit is improved by the addition of generous amounts of garlic, but it is not essential.

Serve the rabbit with winter vegetables, and if you have wild mushrooms from the fields, so much the better.

Chapter Eleven

Health

Ferrets are hardy little creatures, and there is not a lot that goes wrong with them, although once ill, they tend to give up very quickly and die. They have a confusing way of displaying similar symptoms for a variety of ailments: their motor co-ordination fails them, an effect which used to be called 'the staggers'. The back legs lose their use, and the ferret seems semi-paralysed. Sometimes it drags itself endlessly round in circles, as if it has lost its mental as well as its physical powers, sometimes it makes pathetic attempts to reach the latrine corner of the hutch and keep itself clean, despite its failing strength. 'Staggers' is a symptom, not an illness in itself, so if one of your ferrets displays it you must act quickly to ascertain the cause of the problem and stop it spreading to the rest of your stock.

First, isolate the ferret. It is always useful to have a quarantine hutch for foundling, newly bought or ailing ferrets. It should be well away from the others, and so arranged that the ferret has quiet, darkness if required, and complete shelter from the weather. I would recommend that any new ferret is kept away from the rest of your stock for four weeks, to allow any incubating illness to manifest itself. The exception to this is Aleutian disease, of which more shortly.

The first thing to check for is ear mites, the main symptom of which is severe 'staggers', although there is likely to be some head-shaking as well. A mucky, nasty-smelling brown discharge from the ear will confirm the diagnosis. Easily treated with the same ear drops that you would use on cats and dogs, ear mites are a fact of life for ferrets that go down holes, so check your ferrets' ears often. Do not confuse ordinary ear wax with ear mite discharge, however, for a little ear wax is protective and healthy. And do not be tempted to clean your ferrets' ears out with cotton buds, as this can push dirt into the inner ear. A group of ferrets (collectively a 'business') will clean each others' ears; if for any reason you have a solo ferret, you can gently mop out the external shell of the ear with a baby wipe. Ordinarily, ear mites will clear up a day or two after treatment, but occasionally a bad infestation will require two or three sessions. It is not very easy for one person to administer ear drops, but I find that the job can be done quickly if one holds the ferret by the scruff the way its mother would, and administer the drops with the other hand. It is not a pleasant job, so it is best get it over with and then make a fuss of the ferret and play with her for a few minutes until she has forgotten all about it.

Along with ear mites come fleas and ticks, and it is likely that any lost ferret that you find will have some of each. Ticks breathe through their abdomens, and so all you need to do to make them slacken their hold is to coat their bodies with something that will block up the breathing process, such as petroleum jelly, soft margarine or nail varnish. If none of this is to hand, dab on surgical spirit, aftershave, or neat tea tree oil, all of which are safe for the ferret and will loosen the tick. Do not try holding a lighted cigarette end over the tick, as advised by some people: this needs a steady hand and a very still ferret. Do not pull the tick straight off either, as its head will be buried under the skin and will come off as you pull. You will then have the makings of an abscess. Once you have applied the tick-loosening substance, wait a few minutes and then gently ease the whole tick out. Make sure that you kill it, otherwise or it will simply cause trouble again another day.

If your ferrets have fleas, the hutch must be treated as well as the ferrets, otherwise eggs and larvae will remain to reinfest your stock. Fleas seem to arrive in quantity practically overnight. I once brought my ferrets back from a country show infested with red, soft-shelled fleas that gave nasty bites and left itching lumps all over me. Use a mild pet shampoo, lotion or powder which is safe for cats and kittens, remembering that ferrets groom themselves and each other. Steer clear of organophosphate treatments and anything for which you have to wear protective clothing, as these will not be good for your ferrets. I recommend a preparation called Dyna-mite; which is herbal and absolutely safe. If you bathe your ferrets, remember that they are very susceptible to damp and chills, and dry them thoroughly. I towel mine dry, and they chuckle and squirm with delight. I also know of someone who uses a hair drier, which results in a very fluffy ferret! Clean out the hutch completely, disinfect it with a non-phenol preparation, rinse it out thoroughly and allow it to dry before you put the ferrets back in. Alternatively, you can cleanse the hutch with a blowtorch, taking the usual safety precautions.

Sometimes ferrets contract mange – humans can catch it too, in which case it is called scabies – which is best treated by your vet, for there are two varieties and the affliction can become serious in a very short time. Symptoms are persistent scratching, loss of coat, sore and weeping skin and a nasty smell. Do not confuse this sort of hair loss with that which is hormone-induced in an otherwise healthy ferret. In the summer, post-pregnancy or post-false-pregnancy jills will sometimes lose their coats to the extent that they become bald in places, and the excess of hormone in a late summer hob can also cause loss of hair which is usual on the tail. This hormone-induced hair loss is not an illness, and will right itself as the seasons turn and the ferrets moult naturally.

Distemper is a big killer of ferrets, and it is well worthwhile having your ferrets vaccinated against it every year. If your vet is not a ferret specialist, you need to be sure that he or she understands that the canine vaccine is not suitable for ferrets, as it is cultivated on laboratory ferrets. It is rare for a ferret to recover from distemper, so it is not worth taking a risk, especially if you are out and about a lot with your stock. Symptoms are 'staggers', runny eyes and nose, increased thirst, loss of appetite, diarrhoea, often vomiting, and sometimes swelling of the soles of the feet (hard pad). Confusingly, the old name for distemper in ferrets is 'the sweats', which is one thing that they do not do.

Be careful with your feeding, and give your ferrets only the freshest of foods, for they are very susceptible to botulism. This bacterium is present in almost all carcase meat, especially birds, and will proliferate as the carcase decays. Always paunch carcases before feeding, and feed frozen meat as soon as possible after defrosting. If in doubt about the freshness of any meat, either do not feed it or cook it very thoroughly before you give it to your ferrets. Most ferret owners will pick up road kills for their ferrets, as this is a free source of good meat. Never pick up dead squirrels, however, for a squirrel that is dozy enough to get run over may well have been poisoned, and the same applies to rats and mice. Ferrets love eating squirrels, and if you have shot some, or have a squirrel-catching dog, that is fine, but if you have not seen it die, do not risk feeding it to your ferrets. I would not recommend feeding them wild rats, as most have some poison in them, and they carry a variety of unpleasant bacteria.

Some people worry that shot game could give ferrets lead poisoning. This is a fallacy; we have always fed our ferrets quantities of shot game, and ferret mouths are so small that they can spit out the pellets rather than swallow them. If you feed them gunshot carcases, you will simply shovel out the shot when you clean out the hutch.

Your ferrets can catch colds and influenza from you, so minimum contact is best if you are suffering from either. They will echo your symptoms of sneezing, coughing and feeling generally below par, perhaps with a bout of 'the staggers', but remember that respiratory illnesses are more serious for ferrets than for humans, and they could even die. If you have no one to help you look after your ferrets, and you catch a cold or flu, just feed and water your animals, and leave the cleaning out for another day when you are not infectious. Your ferrets are more at risk from your germs than their own.

Check your ferrets' teeth periodically, as they can chip or break, develop abscesses or die at the root. I have also had a ferret get a piece of bone trapped neatly across the roof of his mouth.

Old ferrets are prone to tumours, which may be removed by the vet if they are troubling the ferret. Some ferrets will deal with matters themselves and I once took a ferret to the vet to find that he had bitten off the lump while he was waiting to be seen. Lumps will recur once they have started to appear, and they may possibly turn out to be malignant, but most old-age lumps are benign. Every anaesthetic carries its own risk, and it may be better not to trouble an old and lumpy ferret unless the lumps are affecting its quality of life.

Aleutian disease (AD) is the ferret keeper's nightmare, and has been causing concern in this country since about 1990, although it has been known in mink for much longer. An immune deficiency disease, it is highly contagious, being passed via the placenta from jill to kits, or between adult ferrets via body fluids such as blood, semen, mucus, saliva, urine and faeces, as well as droplet infection from coughing, sneezing or simply breathing. Like other immune deficiency diseases, it can exist in and be spread by an animal which has no obvious symptoms, and which may not develop the disease into the acute stage. The incubation period can extend beyond a year, and the ferret is capable of spreading the disease during this time. Heavy outbreaks of AD were reported in the south of England during 1990-1, with cases evident in many other areas of the country.

Responsible – and heartbreaking – action by ferret owners has resulted in the disease being contained, but it remains a serious worry. AD-positive ferrets must either be killed and the bodies incinerated, or be kept in isolation for the rest of their lives, which involves the ferret keepers being scrupulous about changing their clothes and disinfecting themselves and their clothing after contact with infected stock. AD-positive ferrets must not be used for breeding. It is diagnosed by clipping a toenail from the ferret so that it bleeds, and then taking and analysing a blood sample. This is very distressing for the ferret, and proves nothing except whether the ferret had AD at the time the sample was taken. So beware of buying a ferret that is certified AD-free, as it only means that it was free on the day it was tested; it may have contracted the disease the following day.

Sadly, there is no simple cure to AD. It is certainly possible that the virus has always been present in ferrets in some form, and that unknown circumstances caused it to flare up and spread, rather like the widespread instances of canine parvovirus or rabbit viral haemorrhagic disease, which both appeared suddenly in the early 1980s, and are akin to AD. Exercise caution rather than panicking at this stage: take care with the introduction of new stock, and if you use or own a vasectomised hob that travels out to service his jills, be aware of the dangers of infection. Nowadays, it is better to keep a vasectomised hob purely for use on your own stock. When I judge at ferret shows, I disinfect my hands and the judging table between every ferret; it takes a little longer but is a worthwhile precaution. AD symptoms are similar to those of distemper, but the ferrets lose weight and fade very quickly.

Properly fed on a varied whole-carcase diet, and kept in dry, clean, draught-free housing, your ferrets should remain healthy. For a comprehensive and easy to understand list of ailments and their treatment. I recommend James McKay's book *Complete Guide to Ferrets*.

Chapter Twelve

Conclusion

You can read books and watch videos about ferreting all you like, but nothing is like experiencing it yourself. I have outlined the mechanics of the sport, but you will have to discover the magic for yourself. As you become more proficient, as you are better able to assess which buries are worth trying and which are not, and as you miss fewer hidden pop holes, you will begin to understand the wisdom of dealing with animals, which is that the more you learn, the less you know. These pages give you hints and guidelines, but every ferreting trip is different, and you will see something new every time you go. One of my regular ferreting companions defines a good ferreting day as one where you return with the same ferrets that you started out with, closely followed by any day when you do not have to dig! You will find your own ways of doing things, which may not necessarily conform to other people's ideas, but which will suit you. You might want to keep a ferreting diary to record the things that happen to make each trip different and memorable in its own way, and which, when read years later, brings the day's experiences to life in a way that no mere catalogue of numbers caught ever can.

What is a ferreter? However born and raised, he is a countryman, for there is no ferreting without fieldcraft. Ferreters are a mixed bunch, coming from all sorts of backgrounds. The bramble scratches on the hands of a high-flying executive do not always indicate an interest in gardening. There are also plenty of women ferreters, and if you chance to see a smart person in a smart car stop to pick up dead animal from the road, you may deduce that it is a closet ferreter picking up a gourmet meal for his ferrets. Once in the know, you will look twice at quietly spoken people who tread softly and smell ever so slightly of musk.

Nothing but first-hand experience can convey to you the heart-stopping excitement of hearing the subterranean thunder that precedes the 'whoosh' and 'thump' of the coney in the net, the held breath as a rabbit emerges ear by ear from a bury and looks around, the pride in a dog as she sprints after a rabbit, turns it away from refuge and scoops him up, or the joyful disbelief as you pull off the impossible shot. Ferrets open up this whole world to you, as well as being the most fascinating, cheeky companions, and wonderfully friendly little beasts with which to share some of the finest moments of your life. Can you stay indoors any longer? Hearken to the woods and the fields. Welcome.

INDEX